Exit Strategies
FOR A SECURE RETIREMENT

Innovative financial solutions that protect both
your income and your independence.

STANLEY H. MOLOTSKY
LEE S. MOLOTSKY

Printed in the United States of America

First Printing, 2015

Gradient Positioning Systems, LLC
4105 Lexington Avenue North, Suite 110
Arden Hills, MN 55126 (877) 901-0894

Contributors: Nick Stovall, Nate Lucius, Mike Binger, and Gradient Positioning Systems, LLC

We would like to thank all of our clients, friends and family who encouraged us to put our years of experience helping people manage their money into this book. A special thanks goes to Sharon, Stan's wife and Lee's mother.

TABLE OF CONTENTS

INTRODUCTION 1

CHAPTER 1: *UNDERSTANDING WHAT YOU OWN* 9

CHAPTER 2: *WHACK-A-MOLE YOUR RISK* 25

CHAPTER 3: *CREATING AN INCOME PLAN* 41

CHAPTER 4: *MAXIMIZING SOCIAL SECURITY* 47

CHAPTER 5: *INCOME CREATION TOOLS* 61

CHAPTER 6: *THE DANGER ZONE: IS THE STOCK MARKET
RIGHT FOR ME DURING RETIREMENT?* 79

CHAPTER 7: *WHAT IS MANAGED MONEY?* 91

CHAPTER 8: *NEW IDEAS FOR INVESTING* 103

CHAPTER 9: *TAKING ADVANTAGE OF TAX STRATEGIES* 109

CHAPTER 10: *PROTECTING YOUR ASSETS FROM
FUTURE TAX CHANGES* 121

CHAPTER 11: *ADVANTAGES AND DISADVANTAGES
OF THE ROTH CONVERSION* 133

CHAPTER 12: *YOUR LEGACY BEYOND DOLLARS
AND CENTS* 143

CHAPTER 13: *PREPARING YOUR LEGACY:
WHAT CAN GO WRONG?* 151

CHAPTER 14: *CHOOSING A FINANCIAL PROFESSIONAL* 165

GLOSSARY 181

INTRODUCTION

Christopher's grandfather worked for the same company for nearly his entire career. He had a pension, some savings, and of course his Social Security benefits. When Christopher's grandparents wanted to invest some of their savings, they bought a basic life insurance policy and a mutual fund. There weren't a lot of choices and things were pretty simple. They enjoyed a secure but comfortable retirement and lived to be in their late 60s.

Things are very different today.

Very few of the people Christopher knows have a pension, and saving for retirement has gotten a lot more complicated what with the cost of housing, health care and college tuition thrown in the mix. Both his parents are also still alive, his mom at the age of 84 and his father at the age of 87 and in an assisted living facility. Christopher wonders how long he will live and how he will pay for the rising cost of long term care. Christopher has a 401(k) and an IRA, but he doesn't know what he's invested in or what to expect from year to year.

Will the market go up or down? Will his savings be enough to support him and his wife? Have they done enough to prepare for retirement? Intuitively, Christopher knows it's time to make some changes to his current investments, but he doesn't know how to exit from what he owns. Which investments should he keep and which ones should he change? How much should he sell or move and what will the tax repercussions be? When Christopher talks to his friends and family, it seems they all share the same sentiment: retirement planning is much more complicated today.

DOORWAYS AND DREAMS

As you stand on the threshold of retirement, looking out at what's ahead and speculating about the years to come, you might be filled with equal parts terror and excitement. Retirement is a time in your life of many exits, and making those transitions has gotten much harder and more complicated than it used to be. As you go from working to not working, from drawing a paycheck to drawing down your savings, you also pass through your 60s and 70s and on into your 90s and beyond. You may have dreams and ideas about the kinds of things you want to be doing, but what if you run out of money before those years are over?

Enjoying a comfortable and secure retirement today takes more than just money. It takes solutions, strategies and a custom, tailored plan designed to fit your individual needs. No one knows just how long their retirement years will last or what those years will bring. Will there be a marriage or divorce? College graduations or new jobs? A hurricane? A death? A new baby in the family? As the years go by, they bring about change and movements that set off financial challenges. These challenges must be planned for during retirement in order to exit in and out of these transitions smoothly.

When you are working, it's easier to adapt to the changes because time is one your side, and the money is always coming in. This is what's known in the financial planning world as *the accumulation phase* of your life, because your primary focus during those years is on accumulating assets. What most investors fail to realize when they retire is that exiting the working years and entering into retirement means a change not only in your working habits, but in your money habits as well. As you cross the threshold of retirement, you enter into a new phase of life, a phase known as *the distribution phase.*

Your distribution years are the opposite of your accumulation years. Instead of adding money to the pile, you are taking money out of the pile. Instead of earning, you are spending. Instead of accumulating, you are de-accumulating. **In order for the nest egg you have built to support you for the duration of your retirement, you need a plan for how those dollars will exit your accounts, because you want to distribute the money in the most efficient way possible.** You want to maximize the earning potential of every dollar while protecting your nest egg from market loss; you want to plan effectively for taxes because paying less to Uncle Sam means keeping more for yourself, and you want to plan for the unexpected contingencies and changes that life brings.

Longevity risk is perhaps the largest, unspoken risk not being addressed by retirees today. The longer we live, the longer we continue to take money out of our accounts. Longevity magnifies exponentially any and all other risk including market loss, taxes, inflation and the cost of health care, which can quickly and dramatically drain away your assets.

You can spend your entire life saving and do all the financial planning in the world, but if the issue of longevity and its related contingencies aren't addressed, there's a good chance you will run out of money.

Nothing in life ever stays the same, which is why a good financial plan doesn't stand still. It has many working parts so it can move and adjust to the moving circumstances of your life. When you embark on the retirement planning process, it's an opportunity to rediscover your goals, objectives and your risk tolerance. Working with a qualified financial professional will ensure you have the particular combination of financial tools that match those goals, objectives and risk tolerances. You should always be able to make a graceful exit from any one of your investment strategies, because in the end, retirement should be the time in your life when you get to enjoy your money.

LIVE YOUR RETIREMENT

Preparing for your retirement means preparing to LIVE. You can expect to enjoy more of your golden years than your grandparents did, which is why in our practice, we have developed a planning process and philosophy that takes into consideration the fact that your retirement years could very well last as long as your working years. This makes it a lot more difficult to ensure the durability of your finances, but it's not an impossible task. You can live the retirement you envision for yourself by applying the **LIVE** acronym to your planning process:

L - is for Longevity. Obviously, the longer we live, the more it will cost us. Benefits like Social Security and traditional pension plans are designed to pay out for your lifetime, but how long does your savings need to last? According to the Social Security administration, the average man in 1950 lived to be 65 years old and the average woman lived to be 71. Today, men are living an average of 19 years longer and women an average of 15 years longer, which means if you retire at age 65 today, you need to plan for at least 20 more years of income if not more.* Chapter 5 on *Income Creation Tools* discusses effective investment instruments

---

* *http://www.ncbi.nlm.nih.gov/books/NBK62373/*

that give you the ability to write yourself your own pension for a guaranteed income that can't be outlived.

I - is for Inflation. According to the government's 2.5 to 3 percent quoted inflation rate during the last 10 years, if a person retired 10 years ago with $100,000 worth of income needs, they would need approximately $130,000 today in order to have the same buying power.* Keeping your money in low-earning instruments at 1 or 2 percent may not be enough to help you accomplish your goals. Chapters 9 and 10 will show you how to protect yourself from future inflation and tax liability, and Chapter 11 delves further into a discussion about Roth conversion for an effective way to eliminate income tax on IRA payouts during your retirement years.

V - is for Volatility of the market. Keeping the majority of your money in the stock market in hopes of earning high returns exposes you to the double impact of income withdrawals combined with market downturn. To avoid outliving your money due to market loss, be aware of *the danger zone* and make sure you have a proper exit strategy in place for all your market investments. Chapter 7, *The Danger Zone*, shows you exactly where in the danger zone you might be headed or already located, with a discussion of how the Math of Rebounds directly affects the ability of your investments to last as long as you do.

E - is for the life Events that constantly upset what people are doing. Family issues, health concerns and acts of God can all conspire against the stability of your finances. You may not have control over these events, but you do have control over the allocation of your assets and the investment tools designed to protect and generate income from them. Retiring with security today begins with a sound financial foundation that takes advantage of the multitude of financial tools out there designed to protect you

---

* *http://www.usinflationcalculator.com/inflation/current-inflation-rates/*

and your loved ones in the event of spousal death and chronic illness. Chapter 2, *Whack-a-Mole Your Risk*, sheds light on all the risk your current assets might be exposed to and gives you a somewhat entertaining way to re-allocate those assets in order to increase and rejuvenate income.

NOT A PRODUCT BUT A PLAN

Like Christopher in our story above, fewer and fewer folks these days are retiring with pensions, which means more and more of us are having to create our own plans using the retirement savings we've managed to accumulate. Exiting from our company 401(k) or company stock and moving into financial tools designed to produce steady income is about more than just purchasing an investment product. It's about a comprehensive strategy or plan that can take the money you have, make sure it lasts as long as you do, and help you accomplish your goals and objectives.

You deserve access to the best tool for the job when it comes to your retirement needs, but not every financial professional is qualified for or has access to certain instruments due to the restrictions of his or her employer. We'll go into more depth about this at the end of Chapter 2, *Understanding the Source of Your Investment Advice*, but for now, you need to understand that a lot of financial professionals simply don't have the financial tools you need in stock. They are like a salesperson who can get you a nice sweater in any color, any size, from small, to medium to large. But when it comes to the duration of your retirement years, you need more than just one sweater; you need an entire wardrobe with provisions for cold weather, hot weather and everything in between.

We are Stan and Lee Molotsky, a father and son team with over 85 years of cumulative experience in the financial services industry. As the owners and operators of an independent entity, we have unrestricted access to financial instruments and services, and as a separate and distinct firm, Molotsky Tax Advisory Group, LLC, a Registered Investment Advisory firm, we are held to fiduciary standards of liability. Working together we suggest solutions and design plans that are always in your best interest. There are a lot of people out there who will give you advice about what to do with your money, but not all of them have the ability to offer you a complete plan—with independent and unbiased advice.

THE COMPLETE PACKAGE: TEAM MOLOTSKY

Since 1958, SHM Financial has grown to become a full-service financial planning firm dedicated to wealth protection, tax minimization and comprehensive planning for current and aspiring retirees. Our team of professionals includes an attorney, tax advisors and money managers ready to assist you with the complicated exit strategies that retirement brings. The Molotsky Tax Advisory Group, LLC, is a further expansion of our services, offering professional money management in house or through our strategic investment partner, Gradient Investments, LLC (GI). GI is an SEC Registered Investment Advisor offering clients twenty proprietary portfolios through its strategic investment partners across the country.

Whether you have a lot of savings or just a little, you deserve access to the best possible solutions and a holistic plan designed to alleviate your financial concerns. We offer our prospective clients an initial complimentary/no-obligation risk assessment where we provide independent third-party analysis of your current investments, personalized income projections and ideas which are available for immediate implementation. We look forward to our initial visit and finding out how we can help you get one step closer to your financial goals. Please don't hesitate to call us at 1-800-MONEY-SHM (1-800-666-3974).

Today's retirees are unique individuals; your retirement plan should be no less unique, able to adapt to changing circumstances so you can maintain your independence and achieve your goals. When you work with us here at SHM Financial, you get more than just investment products, you get a complete package. We look forward to helping you customize a plan with unique exit strategies in place, so you can move through with dignity the many doorways and dreams that retirement brings.

- Stanley H. Molotsky, *President and CEO of SHM Financial.*

- Lee S. Molotsky, *Managing Partner of the Molotsky Tax Advisory Group, LLC, a fee based Registered Investment Advisory firm.*

Nothing in this publication is designed to be a recommendation. We cannot make suggestions or recommendations because we do not know your particular circumstances and any financial transaction should only be recommended by a knowledgeable professional who knows and understands your particular situation.

1

UNDERSTANDING WHAT YOU OWN

"Will we have enough money for retirement?"

Will your Social Security benefit, savings and other retirement assets be enough? If you're like Mike and Karen, you hope so. When the couple turned 60 years old, they started thinking about what their lives would be like in the next 10 years. When would they retire? What would their retirement look like? How much money did they have? Was it safe to leave their money where it was, or did they need an exit plan?

They could both count on Social Security benefits, but neither one really knew how much their monthly checks would be, or when to file for them. Mike had a modest pension that he could begin collecting at age 67, but he had always hoped to retire before that age. Karen had a 401(k), but she honestly wasn't exactly sure how it worked, how she could draw money from it and how much income it would provide once she retired.

While Mike and Karen may sound like they're totally in the dark about their retirement, the truth is there are a lot of people just like them. They know retirement is coming and know they have some assets to rely on, but they aren't sure how it will all come together to provide them with a retirement income.

You spend your entire working life hoping what you put into your retirement accounts will help you live comfortably once you clock out of the workforce for good. The key word in that sentiment and the word that can make retirement feel like a looming problem instead of a rewarding life stage, is **hope**. You hope you'll have enough money.

Leaving your retirement up to chance is unadvisable by nearly any standard, yet millions of people find themselves *hoping* instead of planning for a happy ending.

The question isn't CAN you or SHOULD you put your money to work for you and your family. It's HOW.

With information, tools and professional guidance, creating a successful retirement plan can put you in control of your financial management.

WHERE DO YOU START?

Your goals, objectives and your risk tolerance inform your lifestyle and your idea of how you want to live during your retirement years. These are all factors that shape the way you will structure your investments.

To build anything you need to have three things: a plan, the help of a professional and access to the right tools. If you built your house, or bought a house, you probably had a vision of what you wanted, a time frame within which you needed it completed, and the skilled labor of a professional contractor to guide you through the design and build process, or a real estate agent to show you properties that met your specifications. More than likely, you knew what you wanted your house to be like and how you wanted to use the space. You needed the architectural and design skills of a contractor to help give shape to the layout of your home, or the listening skills of a realtor to help select houses that fit your vision. Designing, building, and choosing your retirement follows the same recipe. You may know what you want; a professional with access to a full range of financial tools can help you get you there.

Different financial tools are designed to do different things. Checking and savings accounts provide you with liquid funds to pay the bills; life insurance protects and provides for your loved ones, and accounts earmarked for accumulation such as 401(k), 403(b) or IRAs grow your money for your retirement years. Creating a long term income plan that is both secured and able to grow your money for future needs requires access to multiple financial tools.

Many retirees struggle to find the right investment tools for the job of income creation during their retirement years. Typical interest rates on low-earning investments don't earn enough to keep pace with inflation and taxes, while money left in the market can potentially devastate your retirement income.

It is possible to create your own pension plan using a combination of the right financial tools; what makes this tricky is that the *right tools* will be different for everyone, depending on the specifics of their individual situations.

WHAT DO YOU WANT TO ACCOMPLISH?

When working with a financial professional to achieve a desired outcome, their number one concern should be your goals and objectives. They might ask you, what is the number one thing you want to accomplish as a result of our professional engagement? Would you like to earn more money on your money? Do you want to spend it all while you are alive? Or do you want to pass on money to your grandkids?

As part of a financial discovery, your professional may ask you to prioritize your financial goals. Going through this process can be a valuable way to gain financial clarity. Priority number one might be different for you than for your spouse, and your financial professional should understand and be aware of these differences and the priorities of all parties involved.

Using a ranking system from 1 to 7, assign a number value to each of the following money priorities. For example, if having access to your money is the most important thing to you, then give that box a #1 mark. You only get to use the #1 mark one time, which encourages you to give some thought to what your priorities really are. You won't be limited to or hindered in any way by priority #1 during the execution of your plan, but during the planning process, it's helpful for all involved to be aware of your goals and objectives. They include but are not limited to the following:

- Increase the income generated by your portfolio
- Increase future income during retirement
- Insure income for life
- Minimize your tax obligation
- Protect your assets from the future cost of health care
- Maximize wealth transfer to your heirs
- Allow ease of access to your money

Your money represents more than the paper it's printed on. It is the embodiment of your time, your talents, and your commitments. It buys the food you eat, the house you sleep in, the car you drive, and the clothes you wear. It also helps provide you with the lifestyle you want to live once you retire.

You have spent a lifetime earning it, spending it, and hopefully, accumulating it. When the time comes for retirement, you want your money to provide you with a comfortable lifestyle and stable income after your working days are done. You might also have other desires, such as traveling, purchasing property, or moving to be closer to your family (or farther away). You may also want your assets to provide for your loved ones after you are gone.

Your income, your plans for retirement, your future healthcare expenses, and the continued accumulation of your assets after you stop working and drawing a paycheck all rely on one thing: You.

The way you approach your retirement impacts your income, the taxes your assets are subject to, your financial stability in the future, and your legacy. It is a truism among financial professionals that one hour of organizing your assets can be worth more than an entire lifetime of working and saving when it comes to retirement, which is why the rest of this chapter is devoted to helping you understand the investments you currently own.

During Work	vs.	During Retirement
Money Comes In		Money Goes Out
Accumulate Money		Distribute Money
Accumulate Money		De-Accumulate Money
Enter		Exit
Longevity Decreases Risks		Longevity Increases Risks*
		Ex. market losses, taxes, inflation, healthcare costs, medical conditions, etc.

*The longer we live in retirement, the longer we continue to "take" money from our accounts ... the more things outside of our control will effect our piles of money, in a negative way ... the less money we will have which means we might very well run out of it. This "longevity risk" is one of the largest RISKS you face during retirement, and most people do not address it.

HOPE SO VS. KNOW SO MONEY

Let's take a look at some of the basic truths about money as it relates to saving for retirement.

There are essentially two kinds of money: *Hope So* and *Know So*. Everyone can divide their money into these two categories. Some have more of one kind than the other. The goal isn't to eliminate one kind of money but to balance them as you approach retirement.

Hope So Money is money that is at risk. It fluctuates with the market. It has no minimum guarantee. It is subject to investor activity, stock prices, market trends, buying trends, etc. You get the picture. This money is exposed to more risk but also has

10-Year Treasury Long-term Fixed Rates

Volatility Index – or *Fear Gauge:* Implied Market Volatility

Source: Yahoo Finance – 12-31-2013. VIX is a trademarked ticker symbol for the Chicago Board Options Exchange Market Volatility Index, a popular measure of the implied volatility of S&P 500 index options. Often referred to as the fear index or the fear gauge, it represents one measure of the market's expectation of stock market volatility over the next 30 day period. (wikipedia.com) The CBOE 10-year Treasury Note (TNX) is based on 10 times the yield-to-maturity on the most recently auctioned 10-year Treasury note. Past performance does not guarantee future results. Some illustrations may show how a market index has performed. An investor cannot invest in an index, although there are some investments designed to mirror index performance. Past performance is not a guarantee of future results.

The VIX, or volatility index, of the market represents expected market volatility. When the VIX drops, economic experts expect less volatility. When the VIX rises, more volatility is expected.

1. *VIX is a trademarked ticker symbol for the Chicago Board Options Exchange (CBOE) Market Volatility Index, a popular measure of the implied volatility of S&P 500 index options. Often referred to as the fear index or the fear gauge, it represents one measure of the market's expectation of stock market volatility over the next 30 day period. (wikipedia.com)*

2. *The CBOE 10-Year Treasury Note (TNX) is based on 10 times the yield-to-maturity on the most recently auctioned 10-year Treasury note.*

the potential for more reward. Because the market is subject to change, you can't really be sure what the value of your investments will be worth in the future. You can't really *rely* on it at all. For this reason, we refer to it as Hope So Money.

This doesn't mean you shouldn't have some money invested in the market, but it would be dangerous to assume you can know what it will be worth in the future, which makes exiting from these investments a tricky prospect. If you are relying on these Hope So investments for your retirement income, withdrawing on these funds during a time of market decline can lead to the rapid depletion of your funds. Investors who retired just prior to or after the Great Recession of 2008 saw their portfolios drop by as much as 50 percent. That drop combined with the distribution of income dollars caused many retirees to rethink their plans. Some had to put off retirement or drastically change their lifestyle. Still others had to secure part-time work. The risk of relying on Hope So investment as your only source of income during retirement is covered more fully in Chapter 6: *Beware the Danger Zone.*

Hope So Money is an important element of a retirement plan, especially in the early stages of planning when you can trade volatility for potential returns, and when a longer investment timeframe is available to you. In the long run, time can smooth out the ups and downs of money exposed to the market. Working with a professional money manager to create rewarding returns from Hope So Money is one tool in the investor toolbox you may want to have access to during your retirement.

Know So Money, on the other hand, is safer when compared to Hope So Money. Know So Money is made up of dependable, low-risk or no-risk money, and investments that you can count on. Social Security is one of the most common forms of Know So Money. Income you draw or will draw from Social Security is guaranteed. You have paid into Social Security your entire career, and you can rely on that money during your retirement. Unlike the market, rates of growth for Know So Money are dependent on 10-year treasury rates. The 10-year treasury, or TNX, is commonly considered to represent a very secure and safe place for your money, hence Know So Money. The 10-year treasury drives key rates for things such as mortgage rates or CD rates. Know So Money may not be as exciting as Hope So Money, but it is safer. You can safely be fairly sure you will have it in the future.

Knowing the difference between Hope So and Know So Money is an important step towards a successful retirement plan. People who are 55 or older and who are looking ahead to retirement should be relying on more Know So Money than Hope So Money.

Ideally, the rates of return on Hope So and Know So Money would have an overlapping area that provided an acceptable rate of risk for both types of money. In the early 1990s, interest rates were high and market volatility was low. At that time, you could invest in either Hope So or Know So Money options because the rates of return were similar from both Know So and Hope So investments, and you were likely to be fairly successful with a wide range of investment options. At that time, you could expose yourself to an acceptable amount of risk or an acceptable fixed rate. Basically, it was difficult to make a mistake during that time period. Today, you don't have those options. Market volatility is at all-time highs while interest rates are at all-time lows. They are so far apart from each other that it is hard to know what to do with your money.

Yesterday's investment rules may not work today. Not only could they hamper achieving your goals, they may actually harm your financial situation. We are currently in a period when the rates for Know So Money options are at historic lows, and the volatility of Hope So Money is higher than ever. There is no overlapping acceptable rate, making both options less than ideal.

Because of this uncertain financial landscape, wise investment strategies are more important now than ever.

INSIDER INVESTMENT REPORTS

There are many reasons why you might be uncertain as to how much risk your investments are actually exposed to. In some cases, it's simply a matter of timing: the investments you purchased 20 years ago might have been appropriate investment tools during the accumulation phase of your life, but now as you near or begin retirement, your risk tolerance and objectives have changed. You want to have more Know So investments to secure your retirement income, and you need a plan for your Hope So money to ensure longevity of your funds. You also want to have exit strategies built into every investment in order to give you more flexibility, control and independence.

To begin, it's helpful to organize your assets so you can have a clear understanding of how much of your money is at risk and how much is in safer holdings. This process starts with listing all your assets.

Let's take a look at the two kinds of money:

Hope So Money is, as the name indicates, money that you *hope* will be there when you need it. Hope So Money represents what you would like to get out of your investments. Examples of Hope So Money include:
- Stock market funds, including index funds
- Mutual funds
- Variable annuities
- REITS

Know So Money is money that you know you can count on. It is safer money that isn't exposed to the level of volatility as the asset types noted above. You can more confidently count on having this money when you need it. Examples of Know So Money are:

- Government backed bonds
- Savings and checking accounts
- Fixed income annuities
- CDs
- Treasuries
- Money market accounts

There are also several reports or tests a financial professional can run for you in order to help assess the performance of your current investments. These investment reports are like an x-ray that give you access to the internal bones and workings of an investment using sophisticated computer algorithm software. Other reports examine efficiency and areas of overlap in order to determine the health of your current investments and strategies. These reports include but are not limited to: the Morningstar Report, Custom Annuity Report, Social Security Optimization Report, Wealth Management Report, Roth IRA Conversion Report, Beneficiary Review, and a Tax Preparation Review. Let's take a brief look at how these reports can give you the inside scoop on your investments.

The Morningstar Report: This comprehensive report gives a bird's eye view of your investments. It looks at how a portfolio is currently designed, its current performance, and how it may perform in the future.

The Social Security Optimization Report: If you have questions about how to get the most out of this lifetime benefit, this is an indispensable report that runs through thousands of different filing combinations. By plugging in your information, it does the hard calculations for you, alerting you to the exact month and year to claim your benefit for the maximum lifetime amount of money.

The Custom Annuity Report: This five or six page report breaks apart the internal costs and factors of an annuity contract. For annuity owners, it provides an opportunity to look under the hood of your annuity, so to speak, so you can see the internal workings of current fees and annuitization payouts—an excellent x-ray of your existing annuities.

The Wealth Management Report: For those with larger portfolios, this extensive 15- to 20-page report evaluates the inner workings of portfolios valued at $500,000 or more. This report gives you an insider view detailing asset performance and future performance predictions, as well as identifying areas of overlap, redundancy and inefficiency. It breaks apart the internal workings of different brokerage accounts and Exchange Trade Funds (ETFs) to show you their consistency: how well or poorly they have performed and the holdings and brokerage entities holding said funds. This last part is especially helpful because oftentimes investors aren't aware of the tremendous duplication that can occur inside or under the hood of their portfolio. They might think they are diversified when they really aren't.

Another important thing to know with respect to managed funds is management tenure. This refers to the experience of the professionals managing your money. How long have they been doing what they are doing? Does their track record show performance ratings through various cycles? Good and bad? Do they have the ability to achieve your desired goals and objectives within the parameters of your risk tolerance?

How does your advisor get compensated? How the managers of a mutual fund are compensated for the products they sell can also be discovered during the analysis and review of your current assets. It's nice to know if your financial professional makes money when you make money (compensation based on fund performance), or if they make money whenever they sell you something (compensation based on increased sales of the fund).

In other words, is your fund manager good at growing your money, or are they good at selling you investment products? This is the difference between fee-based and commission-based financial professionals, and there is nothing inherently wrong either way. You just want to be in the know. We will talk in more detail about this subject at the end of Chapter 2.

Taking an insider's look at your current investment portfolio alerts you to areas of non-compliance with your goals, objectives and risk tolerance. Once you've identified discrepancies between what you have and what you need, a few exits might be in order.

> » *Arnold had a modest brokerage account that he added to when he could. When he changed jobs a couple years ago, at age 58, Arnold transferred his 401(k) assets into an IRA. Just a few years from retirement, he is now beginning to realize that nearly every dollar he has saved for retirement is subject to market risk.*
>
> *Intuitively, he knows that the time has come to exit from some of his investments and shift to safer alternatives, but what percentage of his assets should he keep in Hope So Money and what percentage should he move to Know So?*

THE RULE OF 110

Determining the amount of risk that is right for you is dependent on a number of variables. You need to feel comfortable with where and how you are investing your money, and your financial professional is obligated to help you make decisions that put your money in places that fit your risk criteria.

One guiding principal that can help shape asset diversification* for the average investor in the Rule of 110. The original rule, the Rule of 100, states that the number 100 minus an investor's age equals the amount of assets they could have exposed to risk. We have adjusted this rule to reflect the average life expectancy of today's retiree. Adjusting for longevity, we use the Rule of 110.

Asset Diversification disclosure – Diversification and asset allocation does not assure of guarantee better performance and cannot eliminate the risk of investment loss. Before investing, you should carefully read the applicable volatility disclosure for each of the underlying funds, which can be found in the current prospectus.

The Rule of 110: 110 - (your age) = the percentage of your assets that could be exposed to risk (Hope So Money)

For example, if you are a 30-year-old investor, the Rule of 110 would indicate that you could be focusing on investing primarily in the market and taking on a substantial amount of risk in your portfolio. The Rule of 110 suggests that 80 percent of your investments could be exposed to risk.

110 - (30 years of age) = 80 percent

Now, not every 30-year-old should have exactly 80 percent of their assets in mutual funds and stocks. The Rule of 110 is based on your chronological age, not your "financial age," which could vary based on your investment experience, your aversion or acceptance of risk and other factors. While this rule isn't an ironclad solution to anyone's finances, it's a pretty good place to start.

Once you've taken the time to look at your assets with a professional to determine your risk exposure, you can use The Rule of 110 to make changes that put you in a more stable investment position—one that reflects your comfort level. Perhaps when you were age 30 and starting your career, like in the example above, it made sense to have 80 percent of your money in the market: you had time on your side. You had plenty of time to save more money, work more and recover from a downturn in the market. Retirement was ages away, and your earning power was increasing. And indeed, younger investors should take on more risk for exactly those reasons. The potential reward of long-term involvement in the market outweighs the risk of investing when you are young.

Risk tolerance generally reduces as you get older, however. If you are 40 years old and lose 30 percent of your portfolio in a market downturn this year, you have 20 or 30 years to recover it. If you are 68 years old, you have five to 10 years (or less) to make the same recovery. That new circumstance changes your whole retirement perspective. At age 68, it's likely that you simply aren't as interested in suffering through a tough stock market. There is less time to recover from downturns, and the stakes are higher. The money you have saved is money you will soon need to provide you with income, or is money that you already need to meet your income demands.

Much of the flexibility that comes with investing earlier in life is related to *compounding*. Compounded earnings can be incredibly powerful over time. The longer your money has time to compound, the greater your wealth will be. This is what most people talk about when they refer to putting their money to work. This is also why The Rule of 110 favors risk for the young. If you start investing when you are young, you can invest smaller amounts of money in a more aggressive fashion because you have the potential to make a profit in a rising market and you can harness the power of compounding earnings. When you are 40, 50 or 60 years old, that potential becomes less and less and you are forced to have more money at lower amounts of risk to realize the same returns. **It basically becomes more expensive to prudently invest the older you get.**

You risk not having a recovery period the older you get, so should have less of your assets at risk in volatile investments. You should shift with The Rule of 110 to protect your assets and ensure that they will provide you with the income you need in retirement. Let's look at another example that illustrates how The Rule of 110 becomes more critical as you age. An 80-year-old investor who is retired and is relying on retirement assets for income, for example, needs to depend on a solid amount of Know So Money. The Rule of 110 says an 80-year-old investor should have a maximum of 30 percent of his or her assets at risk. Depending on the investor's financial position, even less risk exposure may be required. You are the only person who can make this kind of determination, but The Rule of 110 can help. Everyone has their own level of comfort. Your Rule of 110 results will be based on your goals, objectives and risk tolerance. A financial professional can look at your assets with you and discuss alternatives to optimize your balance between Know So and Hope So Money.

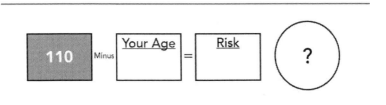

CHAPTER 1 CALL TO ACTION //

- Identify your goals, objectives and risk tolerance when sitting down with your financial professional. What are your priorities during retirement? Do you want to make more money on your money, or secure your income? Rank your priorities to help you and your financial professional determine which financial tools are right for you.
- Notice that the rules for retirement planning have changed. Investing the way your parents did will not pay off and the majority of investment ideas used by financial professionals in the 1990s aren't applicable to today's markets. Keeping your money in low-earning instruments at 1 or 2 percent may not be enough to help you accomplish your goals.
- Understand where and how your assets are invested to secure the safety of your principal. There is money you hope you'll have in the future, and there's money you know you'll have in the future. Organize your assets so you can see what percentages of your savings are invested in risk, Hope So Money and safe, Know So Money.
- Ask your financial professional to run an in-depth analysis report that examines the inner workings of the investments you currently own. One such type of portfolio analysis report is called the Morningstar Report. It examines the inner workings of your investments and compares them to certain benchmarks to capture past and future earnings.
- Use The Rule of 110 as a general guiding principle when determining how much risk your retirement investments should be exposed to (110 - [your age] = [percentage of your investments that can comfortably exposed to risk]).
- Visit the SHM Financial website (shmfinancial.com) to view the video on the Rule of 110 (formerly known as the Rule of 100) from the television show, Molotsky on Money.

2

WHACK-A-MOLE
YOUR RISK

"Have we done enough to prepare?"

If you've ever been to the boardwalk amusement parks along the Jersey shore, or had the opportunity to visit the state fair or a traveling carnival, then you've likely seen the game of whack-a-mole. Little figures in the likeness of moles pop their heads through a spinning ground, and your job is to whack those little moles over the head with a padded mallet. The more moles you can smack squarely the bigger your prize. While whacking fake moles can be a rather satisfying way to get out one's frustrations, it can also be a satisfying way to eradicate your risk and structure your portfolio for growth.

Over the course of your lifetime, it is likely that you have acquired a variety of assets. Assets can range from money that you have in a savings account or a 401(k), to a pension or an IRA. You have earned money and have made financial decisions based on the best information you had at the time. When viewed as a whole, however, you might not have an overall strategy for the management of your assets. Retiring during the challenging financial topography of today's times means it's more important than ever to know which of your assets are at risk. Navigating this financial landscape starts with planful asset management that takes into account your specific needs and options.

Even if you feel that you have plenty of money in your 401(k) or IRA, not knowing how much *risk* those investments are exposed to can cause you major financial suffering. Take the market crash of 2008 for example. In 2008, the average investor lost 30 percent of their 401(k). If more people had shifted their investments away from risk as they neared retirement age (i.e. the Rule of 110), they may have lost a lot less money going into retirement.

In our first meeting, we learn about your goals, objectives and your risk tolerance. In our second meeting, we take a look at what those investments are actually doing for you to see if they in fact align with your priorities during retirement. When you look at your investments in terms of whether or not they align with your goals, you might realize that changes need to be made.

ROCK AROUND THE CLOCK INVESTING

Some investment tools are better suited for income creation while other instruments are more suited for short or long term growth. Still other strategies are designed to provide income, guarantees and growth. To help you decide which investments are the right tool for the job of achieving your retirement goals, it can be helpful to assign colors according to the amount of risk the investment is exposed to.

For our purposes, Know So Money (which is safer and more dependable) is green. A safe Green Money investment is one that is not at risk. It does not fluctuate with the market, which means you don't have to worry, and you can sleep at night knowing your money will be there in the morning.

On the other hand, Hope So Money (which is exposed to risk and fluctuates with the market) is red. A Red Money investment is exposed to the volatility and whims of the market and is not guaranteed. You can lose money in a Red Money investment, but you can also achieve more aggressive gains. While Red Money investments are not designed to be antagonistic, they can be the mortal enemy of the average retiree during the periods prior to and right after retiring, a period of years known as *the Danger Zone*. Losing money due to market loss while in the danger zone puts tremendous stress on the ability of your nest egg to provide sufficient income during today's longer retirement period.

Investing heavily in Red Money and gambling all of your assets on the market is incredibly risky no matter where you fall within The Rule of 110. Money in the market can't be depended on to generate income, and a plan that leans too heavily on Red Money can easily fail, especially when investment decisions are influenced by emotional reactions to market downturns and recoveries. Not only is this an unwise plan, it can be incredibly stressful to an investor who is gambling everything on stocks and mutual funds.

But a plan that uses too much Green Money avoids all volatility and can also fail. Why? Investing all of your money in Certificates of Deposit (CDs), savings accounts, money markets and other low return accounts may provide interest and income, but that likely won't be enough to keep pace with inflation. If you focus exclusively on income from Green Money and avoid owning any stocks or mutual funds in your portfolio, you won't be able to leverage the potential for long-term growth your portfolio needs to stay healthy and productive. This is where The Rule of 110 and a strategy we call Rock Around the Clock investing can help you determine how much of your money should be invested in the market to anticipate your future needs.

The diagram on the opposite page shows different balls in the air divided into different portions of Red Money (risk) or Green Money (safe). Depending on your individual circumstances, you will want to rock around the clock using these circles to adjust your level of risk by applying the Rule of 110. During your working years, for example, you might want 100 percent of your portfolio in Red Money investments so you'd be in the ball at the 1 o'clock position. As you get older, you may want to boogie to a different beat and transition a portion of those assets into safe, Green Money investments. This will help to give you a more appropriate balance of Green and Red Money by helping you gradually exit from your Red Money investments. Rocking around the clock will help to better position your assets so they can help you achieve your personal goals, objectives and risk tolerance.

Visually organizing your assets is an important and powerful way to get a clear picture of what kind of money you have, where it is and how you can best use it in the future. This process is as simple as listing your assets and assigning them a color based on their status as Know So or Hope So Money. Work with your financial professional to create a comprehensive inventory of your assets to understand what you are working with before making any decisions. This may be the first time you have ever sat down and sorted out all of your assets, allowing you to see how much money you have at risk in the market. Comparing the color of your investments will give you an idea of how near or far you are from adhering to The Rule of 110.

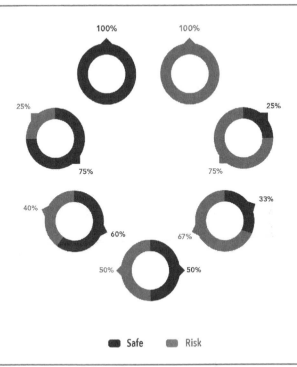

WHACK-A-MOLE BUCKETS

Green Money becomes much more important as you age. While you want to reduce the amount of Red Money you have and to transition it to Green Money, you don't necessarily need all of it to generate income for you right away. This is where using multiple buckets can help you achieve greater growth while minimizing risk, in a strategy we like to call whack-a-mole bucket investing.

There is the money you need for income and money used for accumulation to meet your income needs in five, 10 or 20 years. Money needed for income is Need Now Money. It is money you need to meet your basic needs, to pay your bills, your mortgage if you have one and the costs associated with maintaining your lifestyle. Money used for accumulation is Need Later Money. It's money that you don't need now for income, but will need to rely on down the road. It's still Green Money because you will rely on it later for income and will need to count on it being there. Need Later Money represents income your assets will need to generate for future use. When planning your retirement, it is vital to decide how much of your assets to structure for income and how much to set aside to accumulate to create Need Later Money.

Separating your money into different accounts depending on when you need the money is one way to help you whack down your risk.

During the ten to thirty years that could encompass your retirement years, you're going to experience multiple changes. Because life changes, you need a retirement plan with the flexibility to change with you built in. As fun and crazy as it might sound, the whack-a-mole investment strategy has an exit plan and a way to mitigate your risk built right in.

Each bucket is set for specific period of time, depending on the purpose and need for the money. Your (fun!) job is to tap or whack on each bucket until the money runs out. This keeps the risk moles in check. Because each bucket of money is designed for a specific time period, it also means you are never locked into one single investment for the duration of your retirement. Should you need to change the plan at any point, each bucket also has its own exit strategy or option in place to provide you with the flexibility you need to go with the flow as life changes.

While you are whacking away at one bucket, the money in your other buckets continues to grow. The goal of the whack-a-mole bucket strategy is to end up with the same amount of money in bucket number three as you started with at the beginning.

- Bucket #1: is for your short term income needs for the next 1 to 4 years. This is the bucket where you place your cash reserves, or emergency funds to be used anytime during the next four years. While you whack or spend down this bucket until the money runs out, buckets two and three continue to grow.

- Bucket #2: is a combination of investment tools designed to grow your money for the next 5 to 10 years while you are whacking bucket number one.
- Bucket #3: is the bucket allocated for the long term, maybe 11 or more years. When properly structured, this bucket is designed to grow your money all the way back up to the value of buckets one and two.

For example, let's say we have an investment portfolio valued at $300,000. If we have $200,000 of our funds distributed among buckets 1 and 2, bucket number three would have $100,000 deposited in an investment vehicle designed for long term growth. Objectively, the conservative goal is to grow bucket number three back up to the total value of all three buckets. Under proper management and after 20 years or more, this bucket could conceivably get back up to $300,000.

By using this approach, we've be been able to significantly increase your income during the whacking of buckets one and two, knowing that bucket three is going to be untouched for a good 15 or more years. You are able to have a more generous income by segregating the buckets, and you also have the peace of mind that comes from knowing your income is secured.

RISK MAGNIFIERS: PLAN FOR THE CONTINGENCIES

Risk is about more than just where your money is invested. It's about planning for the contingencies coming down the road. As we mentioned earlier, today's retirees are living longer than previous generations thanks to advances in science and modern medicine. Obviously this is a concern because the longer we live, the more it will cost, and the older you get, the greater the chances that you might outlive your money. About one out of every four

65 year-olds can expect to live past the age of 90, and one out of 10 will live past the age of 95.* As we get older, our bodies get tired and start to wear out, which is why the issue of longevity serves to magnify the already significant concerns in the areas of health and long term care expenses.

The cost of long term care is one area of risk that can quite possibly whack your savings down to nothing if you don't plan for the likelihood of this expense. What happens to your lifetime savings if you need surgery or costly medication? What happens if you or your spouse is diagnosed with a degenerative disease such as Alzheimer's? The Congressional Budget Office reported in 2004 that seniors in general are not prepared for the costs of long term care, citing a cost of $66,000 annually for a private room in a nursing home.** More recent figures from a Genworth 2014 Cost of Care Survey for the state of New Jersey cite an average cost for a semi-private room in a nursing home as high as $109,500 annually, with a private room commanding as much as $118,625.*** And how long will you need this type of care? According to the State of New Jersey's Ombudsman's office, the average length of stay in a long term care facility is 2.5 years.****

Now before you dismiss these figures, understand that long-term care isn't restricted to a stay in a nursing home. It can include personal care for the basic Instrumental Activities of Daily Living (IADLs), such as cooking, cleaning, laundry, or bill paying. As we age, it becomes increasingly difficult to perform simple daily tasks. Menial custodial chores such as taking out the garbage and other necessities can get harder to do, especially when living alone or with a chronic illness. A person hired for this type of home

---

* http://ssa.gov/planners/lifeexpectancy.htm
** http://www.cbo.gov/publication/15584
*** https://www.genworth.com/long-term-care-insurance/nj/get-the-facts/cost.html
**** http://www.state.nj.us/dobi/ins_ombudsman/ltcguide.htm

care performs these IADL activities such as driving and shopping for groceries; they can also assist with bathing, cooking, and housekeeping. Home health care providers, on the other hand, are qualified to dispense medical care and advice. In the state of New Jersey, the current average for adult home care that includes personal care and homemaker services ranges from $22,600 to $48,345 annually depending on full or part-time hours.*

Most people don't enjoy talking about long term care, assisted care and home health care, but if it's not addressed, who is going to take care of it? Long term care is an unpleasant subject to dwell upon, but planning for this reality not only helps preserve your assets, it's one way you can maintain your independence.

» *Emily had $100,000 in a bank CD that was earning 1 percent. After meeting with a financial professional, she became aware of the likelihood that she would need long term care. Both her daughters lived busy lives raising their young children, and Emily didn't want to become a burden to her family. After talking this over with her husband, Emily used that $100,000 to purchase an asset based care product from a life insurance carrier. This product allowed her to earn more money on her money, while at the same time giving her the potential for an income increase should she need long term care. If she never needed long term care, then her husband would receive a $200,000 death benefit. The program also offered a return of investment after a certain number of years, meaning Emily could get her money back should her circumstances ever change.***

---

* *https://www.genworth.com/long-term-care-insurance/nj/get-the-facts/cost.html*
** *Program based on age, insurability and company availability.*

EASY AS ABC: ASSET BASED CARE

Not planning for the inevitabile issues of health care expenses can devastate your retirement savings and drastically reduce your options during your retirement years. *Statistics reveal that 70 percent of retirees age 65 today will need some form of long term care, and 20 percent of those cases will require care for five years or longer.** If these expenses are planned for ahead of time, during the income-planning phase of retirement, you have a lot more options when it comes to paying for them.

Paying for the cost of long term care can be as easy as ABC using Asset Based Care programs and instruments implemented during the planning process. In our story example above, Emily found she could actually earn more money on her money while also securing a source of funds should she ever need long term care. Unlike traditional long term care insurance, if Emily never needs long term care, the money will pass on to her husband or beneficiaries in the form of a death benefit. She is also given an exit strategy so she can get her money out of the investment should her circumstances ever change.

Asset Based Care programs from life insurance carriers offer retirees multiple options, including both Living Benefits and Death Benefits built right into the policy. A Living Benefit refers to a benefit you don't have to die in order to receive, meaning you are able to enjoy the benefits of your money while you are still alive. The plan provides you with the means to pay for home health care or a nursing home facility, in addition to the death benefit protection of a life insurance policy. This gives both you and your spouse more options, control and peace of mind.

Many of today's annuity products also offer long term care options in the form of a rider that provides increased income in the event of chronic illness. This benefit is also known as a home

---

* *http://longtermcare.gov/the-basics/how-much-care-will-you-need/*

health care doubler, impairment doubler or an income doubler because the fixed income contracted by the rider will double or increase should you or your spouse require long term care. The inability to perform two out of the six Activities of Daily Living (ADLs) triggers the benefit, which can also include funding for the basic custodial services mentioned above.

Unlike traditional long term care insurance, with asset based care, the money is not lost if there is no need for the long term care, since the policy also provides a death benefit. You also have more control over the type of care you receive, because when the insurance company pays out the money, you get to control how your money is spent.

» *Irene was a 95 year old woman living in North Jersey who had a daughter and son living in South Jersey. Although Irene still had full cognizant and reasoning abilities, she needed help getting around. Cooking and cleaning the house were things she needed assistance with, but Irene was adamant that she stay in her own home. Her kids wanted her to have her independence, so they hired part-time help and shared the $4,000 a month expense.*

Every week they took turns driving up to North Jersey to check on their mom, until one day the son, Adam, suggested they meet with his financial professional. Together we went over Irene's assets. Adam and his sister both stood to inherit the house when Irene passed away, but the $4,000 a month to pay for her care was already becoming a strain on their resources and family obligations. We noticed that Irene's home was currently worth $450,000 and there was no mortgage on the property. It was suggested they take out a reverse mortgage, and use those funds to pay for the cost of their mom's care. That way, neither sibling had to pay out of pocket, and Irene was able to draw down her own money while she was still alive.

Irene got to stay home and increase her care from part to full time. She was able to stay in her own home and maintain her independence without being a burden to her son or daughter.

GETTING YOUR HOME TO PAY YOU

Staying in your home and hiring in-home nursing care not only saves you money, but for people like Irene, it's also the preferable option. The best way to fund the cost of long term care will depend on your life expectancy, existing health concerns and your current financial situation, but knowing all your options can help make sure you get the financial tool that best fits your goals. One such tool in the toolbox is the equity in your own home.

Reverse mortgages can provide a relatively safe solution to fund the cost of long term care by allowing you to cash in on one of the most valuable resources you have: home. If you are a homeowner age 62 or older, a reverse mortgage allows you the option of converting the equity you have built up in the value of your home into tax-free funds. Retirees like Irene in our story above can reap the rewards of a lifetime investment in homeownership by utilizing the equity built up in their home as a resource to provide financial security. Instead of making payments, you can choose to receive them. Instead of writing that check every month to the bank, the bank gives you the payment. That's the "reverse" part of a reverse mortgage.

A reverse mortgage doesn't have to be considered a last resort. In some cases, such as in the story above, it simply makes good sense. There are a couple of different ways you can set up a reverse mortgage, and this is not a financial solution for everyone. It is your kids who pay for the reverse mortgage, because in the end, they are the ones who stand to get less inheritance. But what a reverse mortgage does best is to provide a way for *you* to access your money now so you can live better during your retirement.

It's up to you to decide if this is a solution that works best for your situation and supports your retirement goals and objectives.

There are requirements you must meet before qualifying for a reverse mortgage. For further information or to see if you qualify, call the number of our HUD reverse mortgage specialist located in the Call to Action section at the end of this chapter. This number will get you direct access to a qualified agent to find out if a reverse mortgage could help you.

WORKING WITH A PROFESSIONAL: UNDERSTANDING THE SOURCE OF YOUR INVESTMENT ADVICE

Essentially, managing your money and your investments is an ongoing process that requires customization and adaptation to a changing world. And make no mistake; the world is always changing. What worked for your parents or even your parents' parents was probably good advice back then. People in retirement or approaching retirement today need new ideas and professional guidance.

In the financial services industry, there are generally two ways of obtaining financial advice: one is given by agents known as registered representatives or brokers, and the other is given by registered investment advisors. These are the people in whose hands you are putting the security of your future, which is why it's vital to your peace of mind to understand how they are compensated for the advice and services they provide. How they get paid is directly linked to the legal standard or code of conduct these professionals are held to.

- Registered representatives or brokers are held to *suitability* standards.
- Registered investment advisors have a *fiduciary* duty to act in the best interests of their clients at all times.

Operating under fiduciary standards, financial professionals are obligated to act in good faith and with candor and to make recommendations that are always in the client's best interest.

The National Association of Personal Financial Advisors (NAPFA) describes financial professionals held to fiduciary standards as occupying a position of special trust and confidence because they are required to act with undivided loyalty.* This includes disclosure of how the financial advisor is to be compensated.

On the other hand, registered representatives or brokers are ethically bound to make product recommendations based on their *suitability* for the client. They aren't required to act in the client's best interest, nor are they prohibited from recommending products that pay out the highest fees to them, as long as those products could be said to be suitable. Brokers get paid a commission based on the products they sell that are affiliated with their firm or company, which means if their company doesn't carry a particular product, they can't offer it to you as a solution. Suitability isn't wrong; it just may not be the best fit for retirees who are entering into their distribution phase. In other words, what was *suitable* during your earning years can actually be harmful to pre- and post-retirees.

Unless your professional works for an independent firm, their access to financial instruments will be limited to the restrictions of his or her employer. As mentioned earlier, registered representatives and brokers are more like sales people who can get you a sweater in any color, any size, as long as they have it in stock. On the other hand, an independent registered investment advisor has unrestricted access to a virtual wardrobe of choices. Not only can they get you a sweater, but they can find slacks and shoes to match. As a retiree facing the daunting task of structuring funds to support their income needs for the next 30 or so years, you

---

* *http://www.napfa.org/about/FiduciaryOath.asp*

need more than just a handful of individual products. You need integrated solutions and you need a plan.

A registered investment advisory firm with access to a team of professionals can put together a comprehensive investment strategy by choosing the financial instruments that best fit your individual goals, objectives and risk tolerance. They are not limited in the choice of products they offer, and their compensation is fee-based as a percentage of assets managed, *not* on products sold. This ensures that the appropriate investment solutions are chosen based on the client's best interest and not on the commission generated.

Most retirees fail to understand the source of the investment advice they are given. Ask yourself, do you want to work with a professional who recommends investment products and strategies that are in their best interest, or yours? What's at stake here is your security and independence.

CHAPTER 2 CALL TO ACTION //

- Assign colors to your investments to help you more easily visualize the assets that make up your retirement savings. Green Money is safer and more reliable; Red Money represents assets that are exposed to risk. Separating your money into different buckets set for different periods of growth is one way to whack down your risk.

- Visit the SHM Financial website (shmfinancial.com) to view the video on Red Ball/Green Ball from the television show, Molotsky on Money.

- Address longevity issues early on during your retirement planning process. ASSET BASED CARE solutions include annuities and newer life insurance policies that specify a Living Benefit. Asset based care solutions can provide the insured with an increased payment each month to help defray the costs of long term care, and if the care is never needed, the policy will pay the benefit to your beneficiaries.

- Determine if you can qualify for certain long term care programs offered through various life insurance carriers by calling 1-800-MONEY-SHM (1-800-666-3974) for a specific overview.

- Consider a reverse mortgage if you are age 62 or older and you need income now or in the future to help pay for expenses such as the cost of long term care. Reverse mortgages are available to U.S. citizens age 62 or older who own and currently live in their existing home.

- Call 1-855-HUD-REVERSE (1-855-483-7383) to find out more information about reverse mortgages and if this program could help you. This number will get you direct access to a qualified agent.

- Understand the source of the investment advice you are given. A professional held to fiduciary standards is legally bound to recommend products that are in your best interest. A professional held to suitability standards is not prohibited from recommending products that pay out the highest fees to him or her, as long as those products are "suitable." Suitability isn't wrong; it just may not be the best fit for retirees.

3

CREATING AN
INCOME PLAN

How much money do we need?

Income is at the very heart of retirement planning. As a retiree, you want your income plan to reflect your individual goals and provide contingencies for the unexpected. How much income do you need every month? And how long must that income last? ***The number one job of your financial plan is to provide you with income during your retirement.*** Doing that requires that you first identify both your current and future expenses, and any gap there might be between those needs and what you have coming in each month.

HOW MUCH DO YOU NEED?

How much money do you need to meet your daily needs? Expense planning begins with your day-to-day needs.

- What is your lifestyle today?
- Would you like to maintain it into retirement?
- Are you meeting your needs?
- Are you happy with your lifestyle?
- What do you really *need* to live on when you retire?
- Do you have a mortgage or rent to pay?
- What are the expenses you currently have that can't be changed?

Some people will have the luxury of maintaining or improving their lifestyle, while others may have to make decisions about what they need versus what they want during their retirement. How much money do you need? **While this amount will be different for everyone, the general rule of thumb is that a retiree will require 70 to 80 percent of their pre-retirement income to maintain their lifestyle.** Once you know what that number is, the key becomes matching your income need with the correct investment tools to satisfy that need.

Once you have identified your current expenses, your next step is to identify when you need the money.

WHEN DO YOU NEED YOUR INCOME?

Creating an income plan that lasts as long as you do requires careful planning for 10, 15, and sometimes even 30 years down the road. That's a lot of dollars.

- What major life events do you anticipate down the road?
- Will you be helping to pay the nursing home costs of a family member?
- Will you be inheriting any property or money?
- Will you be helping to pay for the cost of college tuition?

- How will you pay for your health care expenses?
- Have you made provisions for long term care?

If you need your income to last you 10 years, you will want to use an investment tool that creates just that. If you need a lifetime of income, seek a tool that will provide that, making sure to consider how your income needs might change in the event of spousal death. There are certain life insurance carriers that address the longevity concerns of today's retirees by offering joint payout options for both you and your spouse, regardless of how many years you live. We will talk more in depth about how to create an income stream in Chapter Five: *Income Creation Tools.*

So how do you figure out how much you need and when you need it? When you take longevity, health care costs, and life events into account, you can really give your calculator a workout. This is why Green Money becomes much more important as you age, and where your *whack-a-mole buckets* come into play.

By dividing your assets into different buckets and financial instruments based on time and income needs, any money left over can be set for longer periods of growth. As the years go by, the money in each bucket is whacked on or tapped until that bucket is empty; meanwhile, the other buckets are allowed to grow, thus increasing your growth while preserving access to income. The bucket strategy also allows for greater flexibility, giving you an exit plan should your income needs change at any point. The investments designed for each bucket depend on the individual goals, objectives and risk tolerance of each investor.

WHAT IS THE INCOME GAP?

The moment your working income ceases and you start living off the money you've set aside for retirement is referred to as the **Retirement Cliff**. You've worked and earned money your whole life, but the day that you retire, that income comes to an end. That's the day that you have to rely on your assets to generate income for you. When you begin drawing income from your retirement assets, you have entered the distribution phase of your financial plan. *The distribution phase of your retirement plan* is when you reach the point of relying on your assets for income. This is where your Green Money comes into play: the safer, more reliable assets that you have accumulated that are designed to provide you with a steady income.

After you have calculated your income needs, you will then look to guaranteed sources of money that you can rely on during your retirement. What do you know you have coming in every month?

- Will you be receiving a pension?
- Do you have any rental income?
- Will you be receiving wages from a part time job?
- What will you be receiving from Social Security?
- Do you have any other sources of reliable, guaranteed income?

If your monthly Social Security check and your other supplemental income leaves a shortfall, this is called the **Income Gap.** It needs to be filled in order to maintain your lifestyle into retirement. Ideally, you want to know how to fill that income gap with the fewest dollars possible by decreasing the risk to your Red Money investments and maximizing the returns on your safe, Green Money accounts. Sometimes your home can also be used as a source to generate income. You basically want to buy that income gap for the least amount of money possible. You don't want it to cost you too much, because you want to get the most out of your other assets, including planning for your future and planning for your legacy.

Maximizing your Social Security benefit is where your income starts. Once you have calculated your Social Security benefit and selected the year and month that will maximize your lifetime benefits, it's time to look at your retirement assets that can reduce or eliminate the drop off of the Retirement Cliff. You may have a pension, an IRA or Roth IRA, dividends from stock holdings, or money from the sale of real estate. Filling the income gap begins with balancing your Red and Green Money investments and leveraging your additional assets and retirement saving accounts. Your specific needs, of course, should be analyzed by a professional.

CHAPTER 3 CALL TO ACTION //

- Build your retirement income from the sound foundation of Green Money, or Know So Money. The foundation of a retirement strategy depends on knowing how much money you need for day-to-day expenses and how much you need for future expenses.
- Create an income plan based on how much money you need and when you need it. Using multiple buckets can help you achieve both growth and safety. Using Green, Know So investment to secure your income can free up the rest of your money for growth focused investments that can generate more aggressive returns for future needs. Unexpected expenses such as long term care expenses and life events can devastate your retirement savings if not planned for carefully.
- Calculate your income gap after Social Security and any additional income is accounted for. The difference between the amount you have and the amount you need to meet your needs is called the *Income Gap*.
- Visit the SHM Financial website (shmfinancial.com) to view the Financial Overview video from the television show, Molotsky on Money.

4

MAXIMIZING SOCIAL SECURITY

When should I start taking my Social Security?

Social Security started in 1935 as a way to provide a back-up system to your retirement income needs. At that time, the average life expectancy was the age of 62, and you collected your Social Security benefit at the age of 65. Just looking at those numbers tells you why things are very different today. As people are living longer, their income needs become greater. Learning how to optimize your Social Security benefits is one way to increase the value of one lifetime benefit you have already earned.

There are thousands of choices and combinations when it comes to the timing of your filing. Even if you have already started claiming your benefits, it might not be too late to maximize the lifetime benefits that Social Security can provide for your family.

Here are some facts that illustrate how Americans currently use Social Security:

- 90 percent of Americans age 65 and older receive Social Security benefits.*
- Social Security provides 39 percent of income for retired Americans.*
- Claiming Social Security benefits at the wrong time can reduce your monthly benefit by up to 57 percent.**
- 43 percent of men and 48 percent of women claim Social Security benefits at age 62.**
- 74 percent of retirees receive reduced Social Security benefits.**
- In 2013, the average monthly Social Security benefit was $1,261. *The maximum benefit for 2013 was $2,533. The $1,272 monthly benefit reduction between the average and the maximum is applied for life.****

There are many aspects of Social Security that are well known and others that aren't. Experts spend their entire careers understanding and analyzing it. Luckily, you don't have to understand all of the intricacies of Social Security to maximize its advantages. You simply need to know the best way to manage your Social Security benefit. Taking the time to create a roadmap for your Social Security strategy will help ensure that you are able to exact your maximum benefit and efficiently coordinate it with the rest of your retirement plan.

---

* http://www.ssa.gov/pressoffice/basicfact.htm
** When to Claim Social Security Benefits, David Blanchett, CFA, CFP* January, 2013
*** http://www.socialsecurity.gov/pressoffice/factsheets/colafacts2013.com

UNDERSTANDING THE BASICS OF SOCIAL SECURITY

There are many aspects of Social Security that you have no control over. You don't control how much you put into it, and you don't control what it's invested in or how the government manages it. However, you do control when and how you file for benefits. The real question about Social Security that you need to answer is, "When should I start taking Social Security?" While this is the all-important question, there are a couple of key pieces of information you need to track down first.

Before we get into a few calculations and strategies that can make all the difference, let's start by covering the basic information about Social Security which should give you an idea of where you stand. Just as the foundation of a house creates the stable platform for the rest of the framework to rest upon, your Social Security benefit is an important part of your overall retirement plan. The purpose of the information that follows is not to give an exhaustive explanation of how Social Security works, but to give you some tools and questions to start understanding how Social Security affects your retirement and how you can prepare for it.

Let's start with eligibility.

Eligibility. Understanding how and when you are eligible for Social Security benefits will help clarify what to expect when the time comes to claim them.

To receive retirement benefits from Social Security, you must earn eligibility. In almost all cases, Americans born after 1929 must earn 40 quarters of credit to be eligible to draw their Social Security retirement benefit. In 2013, a Social Security credit represents $1,160 earned in a calendar quarter. The number changes as it is indexed each year, but not drastically. In 2012, a credit represented $1,130. Four quarters of credit is the maximum number that can be earned each year. In 2013, an American would have had to earn at least $4,640 to accumulate four credits. In order to qualify for retirement benefits, you must have earned a minimum number of credits. Additionally, if you are at least 62 years old and have been married to a recipient of Social Security benefits for at least 12 months, you can choose to receive Spousal Benefits. Although 40 is the minimum number of credits required to begin drawing benefits, it is important to know that once you claim your Social Security benefit, there is no going back. Although there may be cost of living adjustments made, you are locked into that base benefit amount forever.

Primary Insurance Amount. You can think of your Primary Insurance Amount (PIA) like a ripening fruit. It represents the amount of your Social Security benefit at your Full Retirement Age (FRA). Your benefit becomes fully ripe at your FRA, and will neither reduce nor increase due to early or delayed retirement options. If you opt to take benefits before your FRA, however, your monthly benefit will be less than your PIA. You will essentially be picking an unripened fruit. On the one hand, waiting until after your FRA to access your benefits will increase your benefit beyond your PIA. On the other hand, you don't want the fruit to overripen, because every month you wait is one less check you get from the government.

Full Retirement Age. Your FRA is an important figure for anyone who is planning to rely on Social Security benefits in their retirement. Depending on when you were born, there is a specific age at which you will attain FRA. Your FRA is dictated by your year of birth and is the age at which you can begin your full monthly benefit. Your FRA is important because it is half of the equation used to calculate your Social Security benefit. The other half of the equation is based on when you start taking benefits.

When Social Security was initially set up, the FRA was age 65, and it still is for people born before 1938. But as time has passed, the age for receiving full retirement benefits has increased. If you were born between 1938 and 1960, your full retirement age is somewhere on a sliding scale between 65 and 67. Anyone born in 1960 or later will now have to wait until age 67 for full benefits. Increasing the FRA has helped the government reduce the cost of the Social Security program, which pays out more than a half trillion dollars to beneficiaries every year!*

While you can begin collecting benefits as early as age 62, the amount you receive as a monthly benefit will be less than it would be if you wait until you reached your FRA or surpass your FRA. It is important to note that if you file for Social Security benefit before your FRA, *the reduction to your monthly benefit will remain in place for the rest of your life.* You can also delay receiving benefits up to age 70, in which case your benefits will be higher than your PIA for the rest of your life.

- At FRA, 100 percent of PIA is available as a monthly benefit.
- At age 62, your Social Security retirement benefits are available. For each month you take benefits prior to your FRA, however, the monthly amount of your benefit is reduced. *This reduction stays in place for the rest of your life.*
- At age 70, your monthly benefit reaches its maximum. After you turn age 70, your monthly benefit will no longer increase.

---

* *http://www.ssa.gov/pressoffice/basicfact.htm*

Year of Birth	Full Retirement Age
1943-1954	66
1955	66 and 2 months
1956	66 and 4 months
1957	66 and 6 months
1958	66 and 8 months
1959	66 and 10 months
1960 or later	age 67*

ROLLING UP YOUR SOCIAL SECURITY

Your Social Security income "rolls up" the longer you wait to claim it. Your monthly benefit will continue to increase until you turn 70 years old. But because Social Security is the foundation of most people's retirement, many Americans feel that they don't have control over how or when they receive their benefits. As a matter of fact, only 4 percent of Americans wait until after their FRA to file for benefits! This trend persists, despite the fact that every dollar you increase your Social Security income by means less money you will have to spend from your nest egg to meet your retirement income needs! For many people, creating their Social Security strategy is the most important decision they can make to positively impact their retirement. *The difference between the best and worst Social Security decision can be tens of thousands of dollars over a lifetime of benefits—up to $170,000!*

Deciding NOW or LATER: Following the above logic, it makes sense to wait as long as you can to begin receiving your Social Security benefit. However, the answer isn't always that simple. Not everyone has the option of waiting. Many people need to rely on Social Security on day one of their retirement. In fact, **nearly 50 percent of 62-year-old Americans file for Social Security benefits.** Why is this number so high? Some might need

---

* *http://www.ssa.gov/OACT/progdata/nra.html*

the income. Others might be in poor health and don't feel they will live long enough to make FRA worthwhile for themselves or their families. It is also possible, however, that the majority of folks taking an early benefit at age 62 are simply under-informed about Social Security. Perhaps they make this major decision based on rumors and emotion.

File Immediately if You:
- Find your job is unbearable.
- Are willing to sacrifice retirement income.
- Are not healthy and need a reliable source of income.

Consider Delaying Your Benefit if You:
- Want to maximize your retirement income.
- Want to increase retirement benefits for your spouse.
- Are still working and like it.
- Are healthy and willing / able to wait to file.

So if you decide to wait, how long should you wait? Lots of people can put it off for a few years, but not everyone can wait until they are 70 years old. Your individual circumstances may be able to help you determine when you should begin taking Social Security. If you do the math, you will quickly see that between ages 62 and 70, there are 96 months in which you can file for your Social Security benefit. If you take into account those 96 months and the 96 months your spouse could also file for Social Security, the number of different strategies for structuring your benefit, you can easily end up with more than 20,000 different scenarios. It's safe to say this isn't the kind of math that most people can easily handle. Each month would result in a different benefit amount. The longer you wait, the higher your monthly benefit amount becomes. Each month you wait, however, is one less month that you receive a Social Security check.

The goal is to maximize your lifetime benefits. That may not always mean waiting until you can get the largest monthly payment. Taking the bigger picture into account, you want to find out how to get the most money out of Social Security over the number of years that you draw from it. Don't underestimate the power of optimizing your benefit: the difference between the BEST and WORST Social Security election can easily be between $30,000 to $50,000 in lifetime benefits. *The difference can be very substantial!*

If you know that every month you wait, your Social Security benefit goes up a little bit, and you also know that every month you wait, you receive one less benefit check, how do you determine where the sweet spot is that maximizes your benefits over your lifetime? Financial professionals have access to software that will calculate the best year and month for you to file for benefits based on your default life expectancy. You can further customize that information by estimating your life expectancy based on your health, habits and family history. If you can then create an income plan (we'll get into this later in the chapter) that helps you wait until the target date for you to file for Social Security, you can optimize your retirement income strategy to get the most out of your Social Security benefit. How can you calculate your life expectancy? Well, you don't know exactly how long you'll live, but you have a better idea than the government does. They rely on averages to make their calculations. *You have much more personal information about your health, lifestyle and family history than they do.* You can use that knowledge to game the system and beat all the other people who are making uninformed decisions by filing early for Social Security.

Let's take a look at an example that shows the impact of working with a financial professional to optimize Social Security benefits:

» Rick and Julia Wilson are a typical American couple who have worked their whole lives and saved when they could. Rick is 60 years old, and Julia is 56 years old. They sat down with a financial professional who logged onto the Social Security website to look up their PIAs. Rick's PIA is $1,900 and Julia's is $900.

If the Wilsons cash in at age 62 and begin taking retirement benefits from Social Security, they will receive an estimated $492,000 in lifetime benefits. That may seem like a lot, but if you divide that amount over 20 years, it averages out to be just shy of $25,000 per year. The Wilsons are accustomed to a more significant annual income than that. To make up the difference, they will have to rely on alternative retirement income options. They will basically have to depend on a bigger nest egg to provide them with the income they need.

If they wait until their FRA, they will increase their lifetime benefits to an estimated $523,700. This option allows them to achieve their Primary Insurance Amount, which will provide them a $33,000 annual income.

After learning the Wilsons' needs and using software to calculate the most optimal time to begin drawing benefits, the Wilsons' financial professional determined that the best option for them drastically increases their potential lifetime benefits to $660,000!

*By using strategies that their financial professional recommended, they increased their potential lifetime benefits by as much as **$148,000**. There's no telling how much you could miss out on from your Social Security if you don't take time to create a strategy that calculates your maximum benefit. For the Wilsons, the value of maximizing their benefits was the difference between night and day. While this may seem like a special case, it isn't uncommon to find benefit increases of this* *magnitude. You'll never know unless you take a look at your own options.*

Despite the importance of knowing when and how to take your Social Security benefit, many of today's retirees and pre-retirees may know little about the mechanics of Social Security and how they can maximize their benefit. While you can and should educate yourself about how Social Security works, the reality is you don't need to know a lot of general information about Social Security in order to make choices about your retirement. What you do need to know is exactly **what to do to maximize your benefit**. Because knowing what you need to do has huge impacts on your retirement! For most Americans, Social Security is the foundation of income planning for retirement. Social Security benefits represent nearly 40 percent of the income of retirees.* For many people, it can represent the largest portion of their retirement income. Not treating your Social Security benefit as an asset and investment tool can lead to sub-optimization of your largest source of retirement income.

MAXIMIZING YOUR LIFETIME BENEFIT

Calculating how to maximize **lifetime benefits** is more important than waiting until age 70 for your maximum **monthly benefit amount**. It's about getting the most income during your lifetime. Professional benefit maximization software can target the year and month that it is most beneficial for you to file based on your life expectancy.

Remember, every month you wait to file, the amount of your benefit check goes up, but you also get one less check. You don't know how exactly how long you're going to live, but you have a better idea of your life expectancy than the actuaries at the Social Security Administration who can only work with averages. They can't make calculations based on your specific situation. A professional can run the numbers for you and get the target date that maximizes your potential lifetime benefits. You can't get this information from the SSA, but you **can** get it from a financial professional.

Your Social Security options don't stop here, however. There are a plethora of other choices you can make to manipulate your benefit payments.

Social Security Benefits For Married Couples:
- *File and Suspend:* This concept allows for a lower-earning spouse to receive up to 50 percent of the other's PIA amount if both spouses file for benefits at the right time.
- *Restricted Application:* A higher-earning spouse may be able to start collecting a spousal benefit on the lower-earning spouse's benefit while allowing his or her benefit to continue to grow. Be clear when you file that you are restricting the application to the spousal benefit only, and not collecting your own benefit. This strategy can help maximize your overall lifetime family benefit, but may not result in the highest individual monthly benefit.
- *Spousal Benefit:* The Spousal Benefit is available to the spouse of someone who is eligible for Retired Worker Benefits. What if there was a way for your spouse to receive his or her benefit for four years and not lose the chance to get his or her maximum benefit when he or she turns age 70? Many people do not know about this strategy and might be missing out on benefits they have earned.
- *Survivorship Benefit:* When one spouse passes away, the survivor is able to receive the larger of the two benefit amounts.

THE DIVORCE FACTOR

How does a divorced spouse qualify for benefits? If you have gone through a divorce, it might affect the retirement benefit to which you are entitled.

A person can receive benefits as a divorced spouse on a former spouse's Social Security record if he or she:

- Was married to the former spouse for at least 10 years;
- Is at least age 62 years old;
- Is unmarried; and
- Is not entitled to a higher Social Security benefit on his or her own record.*

With all of the different options, strategies and benefits to choose from, you can see why filing for Social Security is more complicated than just mailing in the paperwork. Gathering the data and making yourself aware of all your different options isn't enough to know exactly what to do, however. On the one hand, you can knock yourself out trying to figure out which options are best for you and wondering if you made the best decision. On the other hand, you can work with a financial professional who uses customized software that takes all the variables of your specific situation into account and calculates your best option. You have tens of thousands of different options for filing for your Social Security benefit. If your spouse is a different age than you are, it nearly doubles the amount of options you have. This is far more complicated arithmetic than most people can do on their own. If you want a truly accurate understanding of when and how to file, you need someone who will ask you the right questions about your situation, someone who has access to specialized software that can crunch the numbers. The reality is that you need to work with a professional that can provide you with the sophisticated

---

* *http://www.ssa.gov/retire2/yourdivspouse.htm*

analysis of your situation that will help you make a truly informed decision.

Important Questions about Your Social Security Benefit:

- How can I maximize my lifetime benefit? By knowing when and how to file for Social Security. This usually means waiting until you have at least reached your Full Retirement Age. A professional has the experience and the tools to help determine when and how you can maximize your lifetime benefits.
- Who will provide reliable advice for making these decisions? Only a professional has the tools and experience to provide you reliable advice.
- Will the Social Security Administration provide me with the advice? The Social Security Administration cannot provide you with advice or strategies for claiming your benefit. They can give you information about your monthly benefit, but that's it. They also don't have the tools to tell you what your specific best option is. They can accurately answer how the system works, but they can't advise you on what decision to make as to how and when to file for benefits.

The Maximization Report that your financial professional will generate represents an invaluable resource for understanding how and when to file for your Social Security benefit. When you get your customized Social Security Maximization Report, you will not only know all the options available to you—but you will understand the financial implications of each choice. In addition to the analysis, you will also get a report that shows *exactly* at what age—including which month and year—you should trigger benefits and how you should apply. It also includes a variety of other time-specific recommendations, such as when to apply for

Medicare or take Required Minimum Distributions from your qualified plans. A report means there is no need to wonder, or to try to figure out when to take action—the Social Security Maximization Report lays it all out for you in plain English.

CHAPTER 4 CALL TO ACTION //

- Ask your financial professional to run a Social Security Optimization report. Deciding when to take your Social Security benefit is one of the most important decisions you make as a retiree. The three most common ages that people trigger their Social Security benefits are the ages of 62, 66 and 70. In early every circumstance, these ages will not result in the highest lifetime benefit for your family.

- Take control over when and how you file for your Social Security benefit by educating yourself about basic terms such as roll up, FRA and spousal benefits.

- Visit the SHM Financial website (shmfinancial.com) to view video on Maximizing Social Security from the television show, Molotsky on Money.

- If you reside in New Jersey, call 1-800-MONEY-SHM (1-800-666-3974) to arrange for your complimentary Social Security Optimization report.

5

INCOME CREATION TOOLS

"What if you could write yourself a lifetime pension?"

Ed and Sophie are 62 years old and have decided to run the numbers to see what their retirement is going to look like. They know they currently need $6,000 per month to pay their bills and maintain their current lifestyle. They have also done their Social Security homework and have determined that, between the two of them, they will receive $4,200 per month in benefits. They also receive $350 per month in rent from a tenant who lives in a small carriage house in their backyard. Between their Social Security and the monthly rent income, they will be short $1,450 per month.

They do have an additional asset, however. They have been contributing for years to an IRA that has reached a value of $350,000.

They realize that they have to figure out how to turn the $350,000 in their IRA into $1,450 per month for the rest of their life.

At first glance, it may seem like they will have plenty of money. With some quick calculations, they find they have 240 months, or nearly 20 years, of monthly income before they exhaust the account. When you consider income tax, the potential for higher taxes in the future, and market fluctuations (because many IRAs are invested in the market), the amount in the IRA seems to have a little less clout. Every dollar Ed and Sophie take out of the IRA is subject to income tax, and if they leave the remainder in the IRA, they run the risk of losing money in a volatile market. Once they retire and stop getting a paycheck every two weeks, they also stop contributing to their IRA. And when they aren't supplementing its growth with their own money, they are entirely dependent on market growth. That's a scary prospect. They could also withdraw the money from the IRA and put it in a savings account or CD, but removing all the money at once will put them in a tax bracket that will claim a huge portion of the value of the IRA. A seemingly straightforward asset has now become a complicated equation. Ed and Sophie don't know what to do.

After you have calculated your Social Security benefit and have selected the year and month that will maximize your lifetime benefits, you will likely need to find another source of income in order to keep the lifestyle you have grown accustomed to. It's time to look at your other retirement assets, incomes and options that can help fill in your monthly income needs. Like Ed and Sophie, you may have a pension, an IRA or Roth IRA, dividends from stock holdings, money from the sale of real estate, rental property, or other sources of income. But how can these assets be structured so as to provide a protected, guaranteed income stream that grows enough to keep up with inflation and taxes? This chapter will help educate you about the different income creation tools designed specifically to create income during your retirement years.

THE RIGHT TOOL FOR THE JOB

Taxes, longevity and the unpredictability of life events are only three of the many reasons why today's retirees need to rely on more than one kind of instrument when designing an income strategy that can provide durability of income. You do not have the choice of putting more money into Social Security in order to get more out of it. If you *could* have the option to contribute more money toward Social Security in order to secure a guaranteed income, it would be a great way to create a Green Money asset that would enhance your retirement. Since that option isn't available, you may seek an investment tool that is similar to Social Security that provides you with a reliable income. It also has the potential to increase the value of your principal investment! This kind of win-win situation exists, and it's called an annuity.

Income annuities are able to give you a reliable benefit check each month similar to Social Security, but you get to control how much money you put in and when you start receiving the benefits. The returns and guarantees earned by these annuities are usually much better than the low rates earned from other Know So Money investments such as bank CDs, which means you have the potential to grow your principal. And any money left over goes *not* to the insurance company, but to your named beneficiaries.

We have talked repeatedly throughout this book about the importance of having an exit strategy for any investment you own. One large misconception about annuities is that once you put your money in, you can never get it back out. That may have been true in the past, but it is no longer the case today. *Today's annuities can give you a lifetime income stream without annuitization.* What this means in plain terms is that you can still have control of your money even when it's in an income producing annuity. You have access to the funds and are able to make withdrawals (up to a certain amount) without penalty, and you have the ability to exit from the investment and walk away with your money when the annuity matures if you so desire. Multiple annuity products using our bucket strategy gives you even more flexibility and exit options.

Ask yourself the following questions:

- How concerned are you about finding a secure financial vehicle to protect your savings?
- How concerned are you that there may be a better way to structure your savings?

If you are concerned about the best way to fill your income gap, an income annuity investment tool is likely a good option for you. Income annuities have many similar qualities to Social Security that give them the same look and feel as that reliable benefit check you get every month. Most importantly, an income annuity can be an efficient and profitable way to solve your income gap. Consider the following benefits:

Safety and guarantees.

- Tax deferred growth.
- Access to some of your money each year, penalty free.
- A way to eliminate the Required Minimum Distribution (RMD) obligation using certain annuities within an IRA.
- No fees. (Not all annuities have no fees. Be sure to ask your financial professional.)
- A higher return rate than what you can currently get from a bank CD.
- Control over the full amount of your principal.

Today's annuities have been designed to solve problems specific to today's retirees. Even if you've been retired for five years or more, it's never too late to get yourself a pension. Income annuities work very much like Social Security in that they give you that reliable paycheck every month, but that's not all they can do. More than one kind of income annuity exists, with commutation options and income riders that can be added to provide additional benefits and solve more than one problem.

HOW ANNUITIES FIT INTO AN OVERALL INCOME PLAN

In its simplest form, an annuity is a way to invest your money that allows you to structure it for income. Annuities come in a variety of modes. Finding the right one for you will take a conversation with your financial professional. Be sure you fully understand the features, benefits and costs of any annuity you are considering before investing money.

Here is how an income annuity can work:

When you put your money into an annuity, you are essentially buying an investment product from an insurance company. It is a contract between you and the insurance company that provides the investment tool. Let's say you have saved $100,000 and need it to generate income to meet your needs above and beyond your Social Security and pension checks. You give the $100,000 to an insurance company, who in turn invests it to generate growth.

The insurance company will usually select investments that have modest returns over long term horizons. In other words, they generally put it somewhere stable and predictable. Most commonly, they will invest it in a combination of bonds and treasuries that are safer and dependable ways to grow money. They use the money from the insurance products they sell to invest, use a portion of the returns to generate profits for themselves, and return a portion to clients in the form of payouts, claims, and structured income options.

One of the most attractive qualities of these types of annuities is something called annual reset. Annual reset is sometimes also referred to as "ratcheting." Instead of taking on the risk that comes with putting money in a fluctuating market, you can offset that risk onto the insurance company. It works like this: If the market goes down, you don't suffer a loss. Instead, the insurance company absorbs it. But if the market goes up, you share with the insurance company some of the profit made on the gain. The amount of gain you get is called your annuity participation rate. Typically the insurer will cap the amount of gain you can realize at somewhere between 3 and 7 percent. If the market goes up 10 percent, you would realize a portion of that gain (whatever percentage you are capped at). This means you never lose money on your investment, while always gaining a portion of the upswings. The measurement period of your annuity can be calculated monthly, weekly and even daily, but most annuities are measured annually. The level of the index when you buy and the index level one year later will determine what amount you might gain. In a fixed index linked annuity, you never have to worry about a loss of principal.

THE FLEXIBILITY OF AN INCOME RIDER

One desirable optional feature with indexed annuities is the additional purchase of an income rider. Income riders are designed to provide safety of principal and a guaranteed lifetime income to people who are worried about running out of money during retirement. One of their most attractive features is their flexibility. You can still receive lifelong income and stay in control of your account with an income rider when abiding by the guaranteed rules of the policy. Adding an income rider to a fixed or indexed annuity gives you the following benefits:

- the option to exit and cash out the policy
- the option to later purchase a new investment or policy
- control over when to turn on the income stream
- the option of Living Benefits payable to you during retirement
- money for your beneficiaries

It should be noted that some of the older annuity policies without income riders function like traditional pensions in that once you die, any money left in the account goes back to the insurance company. This is not the case with the majority of the annuities offered after 2009.

Here is how income riders work:
When you use that $100,000 to buy a contract with an insurance company in the form of an annuity, you are pegging your money on an index. It could be the S&P 500, the Dow Jones Industrial Average or any number of indexes. **The key to how well these** annuities perform is their ability to track **any one of a number of investment indexes along with the guarantee that you won't lose your principal from a market correction.** What this means for you is that when the market goes up, your money goes up. When the market goes down, your principal stays the same. In other words, you don't lose principal due to market fluctuations. This is known as the power of annual reset: you are able to retain the gains earned from the index of your choice when it goes up, without losing principal when the index goes down.

To generate income from the annuity, you select something called an income rider. An income rider is a subset of an indexed annuity. Essentially, it is the amount of money from which the insurance company will pay you an income while you have your money in their annuity. Your income rider is a larger number than what your investment is actually worth, and if you select the income rider, it will increase in value over time, providing you with more income. As the insurance company holds your money and invests it, they generate a return on it that they use to pay you a regular monthly income based on a higher number. The insurance company has to outperform the amount that they pay you in order to make a profit.

Remember, insurance companies make long-term investments that provide them with predictable flows of money. They like to stabilize the amount of money that goes in and out of their doors instead of paying and receiving large unpredictable chunks at once. When you opt for an income rider, an insurance company can reliably predict how much money they will pay out to you over a set period of time. It's predictable, and they like that. They can base their business on those predictable numbers. Always remember not all annuities are created equal; make sure you understand what you are acquiring and ask yourself whether or not it fits with your goals and objectives. A crucial tenet of our practice is to make sure that you understand the different programs we present, because if you do not understand what you are considering acquiring, it's not something you should do.

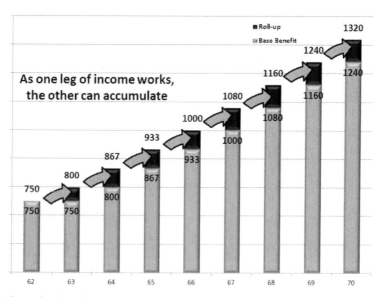

This is a hypothetical illustration

HOW TO MAINTAIN CONTROL OVER YOUR MONEY

In order to encourage investors to leave their money in their annuity contracts, insurance companies create surrender periods that protect their investments. If you remove your money from the annuity contract during the surrender period, you will pay a penalty and will not be able to receive your entire investment amount back. A typical surrender period is 10 years. If after three years you decide that you want your $100,000 back, the insurance company has that money tied up in bonds and other investments with the understanding that they will have it for another seven years. Because they will take a hit on removing the money from their investments prematurely, you will have to pay a surrender charge that makes up for their loss. During the surrender period, an annuity is not a demand deposit account like a savings or checking account. The higher returns that you are guaranteed from an annuity are dependent on the timeframe you selected. The longer an insurance company can hold your money, the easier it is for them to guarantee a predictable return on it.

If you leave your money in the annuity contract, you get a reliable monthly income no matter what happens in the market. **Once the surrender period has expired, you can exit from the annuity and remove your money whenever you want.** Your money becomes liquid again because the insurance company has used it in an investment that fits the timeline of your surrender period. For many people, this is an attractive trade off that can provide a creative solution for filling their income gap.

When is an annuity with an income rider right for you? A good financial professional can help you make that determination by taking the time to listen closely to your situation and understanding what your needs are as you enter retirement. Some people need income today, others need it in five or 10 years. Others may have their income needs met but are planning to move closer to their children and will need to buy a house in 10 years. Or, if you want income in 15 years, you might want to choose a different investment product for 10 years, and then switch to an annuity with an income rider during the last five years of your timeline. Everyone's situation is different and everyone's needs are different. People who are interested in annuities, however, usually need to make decisions that affect their income needs, whether it is filling their income gap, or providing for income down the road.

WRITE YOUR OWN PERSONAL PENSION

One of the most underutilized income creation tools is an immediate annuity is known as the SPIA, or Single Premium Immediate Annuity. As the name suggests, you would choose a SPIA if your income needs were immediate, making it a good choice for bucket #1: income needs for one to four years.

A Single Premium Immediate Annuity is simply a contract between you and an insurance company that allows you to convert a lump sum of money into an income you can start drawing on next month for an agreed upon time period. That time period could be five years, or it could be for the remainder of your lifetime. You might want to think of a SPIA as a mini-pension. They provide an immediate stream of reliable income when you can't afford to take the risk of losing money in a fluctuating market. Income payments from a SPIA can be monthly, quarterly or yearly payments and they can begin the moment you buy the contract.

Today's SPIAs offer an exit strategy using what's known as the commutation value. **A commutation is an exchange of one kind of payment for another.** When designing a comprehensive income plan, the chances of needing the lump sum devoted to a SPIA annuity are rare; however, life events happen and things change. You want to make sure that you have selected a SPIA with a commutable value in order to give you an exit strategy.

SPIAs can also provide a solution to the problem of spousal continuation. If one spouse dies and they have a pension, that income usually disappears when they do. This can leave your spouse with an income cut in half. The following story illustrates how a SPIA with a Joint Life option can work for a retiree.

> » *Miriam's husband, Earl, retires early at the age of 62. He takes the funds he has saved in his IRA and purchases an immediate annuity because Earl doesn't have a traditional pension and his dad lived to be 101. He purchases an immediate annuity with a joint life option so he will get income for the rest of his life and so his lovely bride will also get the money should he meet an early demise. In this investment, his money is guaranteed, and should his circumstances change, he has a dignified exit strategy. If Earl lives to be 110, his annuity will still pay out income; should he die before his wife does, he has the peace of mind knowing that Miriam will receive the income for the rest of her life.*

THREE THINGS YOU NEED TO KNOW BEFORE BUYING A SPIA

Before purchasing a SPIA, make sure you carefully select the guarantee that fits your needs. Oftentimes, people make the mistake of simply choosing the highest lifetime benefit when purchasing a SPIA, but this option may not meet your goals and objectives. There are three guarantees you can put on a SPIA annuity contract:

Option #1: Life Only: Electing the *life only* option on your SPIA means that when the life of the SPIA owner is over, so is the SPIA. The income is paid out to that person for his or her life. The benefit of electing this option is that it provides the highest payout you can get because there is no guarantee. It ends when that person does, whether they live for three or thirty more years. Any money not accessed goes back to the insurance company. Why would anybody ever elect a *life only* SPIA? This option is appropriate for single people or someone with well-to-do children who wants or needs to earn the most money for themselves.

Option #2: Life with Period Certain: This option simply means that you are guaranteed to get out *at least* what you paid in to the investment. This guarantee is often easier because you can readily calculate who is paying out the most money. This also provides you with a principal guarantee. If you meet an early demise, your beneficiaries will receive payments until they get back every dollar you put into the annuity. If you live beyond the guarantee, you will still continue to receive payments, but when you die, there will be no payments made to your beneficiaries because the money you put in was already tapped.

For example, if you have a life with a period certain guarantee of 15 years, and you meet an early demise after only six years, the benefit that would have been sent to you during years seven through 15 are paid to your husband, kids or other designated beneficiary. The longer the guarantee period, the lower the lifetime payment.

In summary: if you live past the guarantee, you still get your income, but your beneficiaries receive no additional funds. If you die prior to the period certain guarantee, your beneficiaries get the remaining money.

Option #3: Joint Life: The third guarantee is often the most desirable and is also known as the "Cash Refund Guarantee". This option gives you more than one exit strategy should you meet an early demise. The joint life option is a good way to ensure your spouse is taken care of should one of you pass away before the other. As in our story example with Miriam and Earl, you can choose to have the annuity pay out for both your lifetimes, or you can choose to have it pay out for only one lifetime. With the one lifetime option, should you meet an early demise and you haven't yet gotten back what you put into the fund, then your beneficiary immediately receive a lump sum payment. This gives them an exit strategy from the investment and more options given the new circumstances.

The bottom line: If you purchase a SPIA annuity for income generation, either for yourself or your family, make sure you have at least one of these guarantees in place.

Additional Annuity Information:

- Some contracts will allow you to draw income from the high water mark that the market reaches each year. The income rider will then begin calculating its value from the high water mark.
- Income annuities are investment tools that look and feel a bit like Social Security. Every year you allow the money to grow with the market, and it will "roll up" by a specific amount, paying out a specific percent to you as income each year.
- Annuities can work very well to create income, and a financial professional can help you find the one that best matches your income need, and can also structure it to work perfectly for you.

MANAGING RISK WITHIN YOUR ANNUITY

Variable annuities are a Red Money annuity that can lose money due to market fluctuations. As their name suggests, they vary with the stock market and the value of the principal is not guaranteed. If you discover that you have a variable annuity as part of your portfolio, you may want to have it reviewed because these annuities are known for having high fees. Because they are connected to multiple mutual funds, there is usually a fee attached to the management of each fund in addition to Mortality and Expense fees (listed as M&E fees) and administrative fees of the annuity.

The cost of these fees are often not easy to identify on your account statements, so many investors fail to consider the true cost of a variable annuity investment.

If your variable annuity has an income rider on it (and you may not even be aware of this,) the Income Account Value will stay the same or grow, but the value of your *actual* contract may fall. If you surrender the annuity, the insurance company will pay you the market value of the asset, regardless of whether it matches, exceeds or falls short of the value at which you bought the contract. If its value has dropped significantly, you may be better off taking the income rider as an income-for-life stream without surrendering your contract.

Just like any investment strategy, the amount of risk needs to fit the comfort level of the investor. Annuities are no exception. Without going into too much detail, here are some additional ways to manage risk with annuity options:

- Remember that variable annuities can lose money with market fluctuations. These annuities do not take advantage of annual reset when the market goes down. The income rider will stay the same, but the value of your actual contract may fall.

- If you want to structure an annuity investment for growth over a long period of time, be aware that the variable annuity option most often does not have principal guarantee protection. With a variable annuity, the value of your principal investment follows the market and can lose or gain value with the market. This type of annuity can also have an income rider, but it is really more useful as an accumulation tool that bets on an improving market. A 40-year-old couple, for example, will probably want to structure more for growth and take on more risk than someone in their 70s. The 40-year-old couple may select a variable annuity with an income rider that kicks in when they plan to retire. If it rises with the market or outperforms it, the value of their investment has grown. If the market loses ground over the duration of the contract or their annuity underperforms, they can still rely on the income rider.

- If you are 68 years old and you have more immediate income needs that you need to come up with above and beyond your Social Security, you need a low risk, reliable source of income. If you choose an annuity option, you are looking for something that will pay out an income right away over a relatively short timeframe. You might want to opt for a SPIA that pays you immediately and spans a five year period, as well as an additional income annuity that begins paying you in five years, and another longer term annuity that begins paying you in 10 years.

- Bear in mind that each annuity contract has its own costs and fees. Review these with your financial professional before you determine the best types of contracts and strategies for your situation.

CREATING AN INCOME PLAN

Creating an income plan before you retire allows you to satisfy your need for lifetime income and ensures that your lifestyle can last as long as you do. You also want to create a plan that operates in the most efficient way possible. Doing so will give more security and will potentially allow you to build your legacy down the road. There are many strategies you can use to maximize the income streams from your annuity. One strategy using a multiple bucket approach involves multiple income creation tools as shown in the following story:

» *Patricia is 60 years old and is wondering how she can use her assets to provide her with a retirement income. She has a*

$5,000 per month income need. If she starts withdrawing her Social Security benefit in six years at age 66, it will provide her with $2,200 per month. She also has a pension that kicks in at age 70 that will give her another $1,320 per month. That leaves an income gap of $2,800 from ages 66 to 69, and then an income gap of $1,480 at age 70 and beyond. If Patricia uses only Green Money to solve her income need, she will need to deposit $918,360 at 2 percent interest to meet her monthly goal for her lifetime. If she opts to use Red Money and withdraws the amount she needs each month from the market, let's say the S & P 500, she will run out of cash in 10 years if she invested between the years of 2000 and 2012. Suffering a market downturn like that during the period for which she is relying on it for retirement income will change her life, and not for the better.

Working with a financial professional to find a better way, Patricia found that she could use more than one tool to fill her income gap. Her professional recommended two different income vehicles: one that allowed her to deposit just $190,161 with a 2 percent return, and one that was a $146,000 income annuity. These tools filled her income gap with $336,161, requiring her to spend $582,000 less money to accomplish her goal! Working with a professional to find the right tools for her retirement needs saved Patricia over half a million dollars.

One very effective strategy for filling the income gap is to put more than one annuity product together in a strategy known as laddering. This strategy is employed using multiple buckets as described earlier, each set for income generation for specific time periods. Using multiple income creation tools can structure income for 5, 10 and 15 or more years down the road and provide for your Need Later Money needs. You can also purchase annuities from more than one life insurance company, allowing you to take advantage of financial instruments that give you the most favorable terms and returns to satisfy your goals, objectives and risk tolerance.

Yesterday's investment rules may not work today. Not only could they hamper the achievement of your goals, they may actually harm your financial situation. We are currently in a period when the rates for Know So Money options are at historic lows, and the volatility of Hope So Money is higher than ever. There is no overlapping acceptable rate, making both options less than ideal. *Because of this uncertain financial landscape, wise investment strategies are more important now than ever.*

CHAPTER 5 CALL TO ACTION //

- Review your income needs and look specifically at the short-fall you may have during each year of your retirement based on your Social Security income, and income from any other assets you have.

- Ask yourself where you are in your payout or income phase. Is retirement one year away? 10 years away? Last year? After Social Security and your additional income is accounted for, the amount that's left to meet your needs is called the *Income Gap*. It's important to find the right investment tool for filling the income gap, because most retirees will live longer than their parents did.

- Determine how much money you need and how you need to structure your existing assets to provide for that need. If you have an asset from which you need to generate income, consider options offered by purchasing an income rider on an annuity. Income annuities participate in market growth without market loss through a strategy known as indexing. Indexing combined with the power of annual reset gives you both growth and the guaranteed safety of your principal.

- Understand the features, benefits, costs and fees associated with any annuity product before you invest.

- Call 1-800-MONEY-SHM (1-800-666-3974) for a complimentary Custom Annuity Report.

6

THE DANGER ZONE
IS THE STOCK MARKET RIGHT
FOR ME DURING RETIREMENT?

Advice about what to do with money has been around as long as money has existed. Hindsight allows us to see which advice was good and which advice didn't cut the mustard. Some sources of advice have been around for a very long time. While there are some basic investment concepts that have stood the test of time, most strategies that work *are able to adapt* to changing conditions in the economy and the world, as well as changes in your personal circumstances.

The reality is that investment strategies and savings plans that worked in the past have encountered challenging new circumstances that have turned them on their heads. The Great Recession of the early 2000's highlighted how old investment ideas were not only ineffective but incredibly destructive to the retirement plans of millions of Americans. Perhaps the most important lessons investors learned from the Great Recession is that not understanding where your money is invested and the potential risks of those investments can work against you, your plans for retirement and your legacy.

WHAT PHASE OF THE GAME ARE YOU IN?

In the game of football, the area 20 yards in from the goal line is known as the red zone. When you're in this zone, not only are you running out of time, but the field is getting smaller. The pressure is on and the last thing you want is to drop the ball. This is an apt analogy for the period during which you transition out of the accumulation phase and into the distribution phase.

The red zone of your retirement are the three years prior to and the three years just after retiring. The football can be compared to your nest egg: to lose all of your savings in the red zone could mean *game over*. The playing field or number of years left to grow your money has been significantly altered, which means that losing money during the danger zone years can exponentially increase your chances of running out of money.

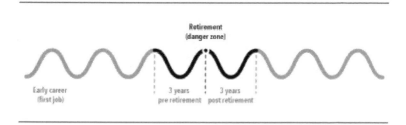

Retirement
(danger zone)

Early career
(first job)

3 years
pre retirement

3 years
post retirement

As the above diagram illustrates, early on in your career you have a long path on which to merrily stroll along. You also have a long path post retirement during which it is possible to utilize Red Money investments for growth or accumulation. But you must be aware of the danger zone that occurs between. To understand exactly why this is true, we're going to talk about the math of rebounds and the sequence of returns.

IS THE GLASS HALF FULL OR HALF EMPTY?

Taking a hit in the market hurts no matter how stable your income, but most people don't realize that, once you have taken that step back, it requires an even larger step forward to return to where you were. You might have the sentiment, "the market always comes back," but even if you do get back to where you were before the loss, your money isn't growing and earning the same way it was before the hit occurred. The math of rebounds, as it is known, uses the percentage of the investment, and not the dollar amount, to calculate what you will need to earn in order to recapture your loses. It also shows us in terms of concrete terms of numbers why market loss is so devastating during the danger zone to the longevity of an income plan.

The following chart shows you the rate of return you would need in order to regrow your money after sustaining a loss:

LOSS	GAIN NEEDED TO BE EVEN
25 PERCENT	33 PERCENT
40 PERCENT	67 PERCENT
50 PERCENT	100 PERCENT

For example, if you had $100,000 invested in the stock market in 2007, and along comes the downturn of 2008, the market takes a reduction of 50 percent. This can be compared to a glass of water where you wonder, is it half empty or half full? The math of rebounds unfortunately points to the reality that your portfolio is half empty. You need to double the amount of money in order to get back to what you had before. Once your $100,000 becomes $50,000, it will take a 100-percent gain to fill you up again.

But wait, it gets even worse.

Losing this money during your distribution years means you will be taking money out of the account in order to provide your income. Regular withdrawals from your account combined with unfortunate market timing can do more than just deplete your savings—it can increase the chances that you will run out of money.

Is the market right for you during retirement? Investors use the term *accumulation* to describe the stacking of interest on top of principal. While accumulation is often desirable during retirement, your appetite for high returns should be tempered by the realities of your timeline and your proximity to the danger zone. Using the bucket strategies outlined in Chapter 2, *Whack-a-Mole Your Risk*, you can secure your retirement income in Green Money investments that are guaranteed, and your growth money is a separate bucket set for long term growth. When a market corrections come along—and they will come along—you won't lose any of the money you are relying on for your income needs. Multiple buckets means you always have an exit strategy so if an opportunity to earn high gains presents itself, you have options.

HOW REAL PEOPLE MAKE INVESTMENT DECISIONS

It can be challenging to watch the stock market's erratic changes every month, week or even every day. When you have your money riding on it, the ride can feel pretty bumpy. When you are managing your money by yourself, emotions inevitably enter into the mix. The Dow Jones Industrial Average and the S&P 500 represent more to you than market fluctuations. They represent your retirement dreams. It's hard not to be emotional about it.

Everyone knows you should buy low and sell high. But this is what is more likely to happen:

The market takes a downturn, similar to the 2008 crash, and investors see as much as a 30 percent loss in their stock holdings. It's hard to watch, and it's harder to bear the pain of losing that much money. The math of rebounds means that they will need to rely on even larger gains just to get back to where things were before the downturn. They sell. But eventually, and inevitably, the market begins to rise again. Maybe slowly, maybe with some moderate growth, but by the time the average investor notices an upward trend and wants to buy in again, they have already missed a great deal of the gains.

> » *Beverly worked for a paper mill company for 34 years. During her time there, she acquired bonuses and pay raises that often included shares of stock in the company. She also dedicated part of her paycheck every month to a 401(k) that bought stock in the company. By the time she retired, Beverly has $250,000 worth of company stock.*
>
> *Although she had contributed to her 401(k) account every month, Beverly didn't cultivate any other assets that could generate income for her during retirement. Beverly also retired early at age 62 because of her failing health. The commute to work every day was becoming difficult in her weakened condition and she wanted to enjoy the rest of her life in retirement instead of working in the cramped office of the paper mill company.*
>
> *Because she retired early, Beverly failed to maximize her Social Security benefit. While she lives a modest lifestyle, her income needs are $3,500 per month. Beverly's monthly Social Security check only covers $1,900, leaving her with a $1,600 income gap. To supplement her Social Security check, Beverly sells $1,600 of company stock each month*

to meet her income needs. A $250,000 401(k) is nothing to sneeze at, but reducing its value by $1,600 every month will decimate her savings within 10 years. And that's if the market stays neutral or grows modestly. If the market takes a downturn, the money that Beverly relies on to fill her income gap will rapidly diminish. Even if the market starts going up in a couple of years, it will take much larger gains for her to recover the value that she lost due to the math of rebounds.

Unhappily for Beverly, she retired in 2007, just before the major market downturn that lasted for several years. She lost more than 40 percent of the value of her stock. Because Beverly needed to sell her stock to meet her basic income needs, the market price of the stock was secondary to her need for the money. When she needed money, she was forced to sell however many shares she needed to fill her income gap that month. And if she has a financial crisis, involving a need for long term medical care, for example, she will be forced to sell stock even if the market is low and her shares are nearly worthless.

Beverly realizes that she could have relied on an investment structured to deliver her a regular income while protecting the value of her investment. She could have kept her $250,000 from diminishing while enjoying her lifestyle into retirement regardless of the volatility of the market. Ideally, Beverly would have restructured her 401(k) to reflect the level of risk that she was able to take. In her case, she would have had most of her money in Know So Money assets, allowing her to rely on the value of her assets when she needed them.

EMOTIONS AND MONEY

In 2013, DALBAR, the well-respected financial services market research firm, released their annual "Quantitative Analysis of Investment Behavior" report (QAIB). The report studied the impact of market volatility on individual investors: people like Beverly, or anyone who was managing (or mismanaging) their own investments in the stock market.

According to the study, volatility not only caused investors to make decisions based on their emotions, those decisions also harmed their investments and prevented them from realizing potential gains. So why do people meddle so much with their investments when the market is fluctuating? Part of the reason is that many people have financial obligations that they don't have control over. Significant expenses like house payments, the unexpected cost of replacing a broken-down car, and medical bills can put people in a position where they need money. If they need to sell investments to come up with that money, they don't have the luxury of selling when they *want* to. They must sell when they *need* to.

DALBAR's "Quantitative Analysis of Investor Behavior" has been used to measure the effects of investors' buying, selling and mutual fund switching decisions since 1994. The QAIB shows time and time again over nearly a 20 year period that the average investor earns less, and in many cases, significantly less than the performance of mutual funds suggests. QAIB's goal is to improve independent investor performance and to help financial professionals provide helpful advice and investment strategies that address the concerns and behaviors of the average investor.

An excerpt from the report claims that:

"QAIB offers guidance on how and where investor behaviors can be improved. No matter what the state of the mutual fund industry, boom or bust: Investment results are more dependent on investor behavior than on fund performance. Mutual fund investors who hold on to their investments are more successful than those who time the market.

QAIB uses data from the Investment Company Institute (ICI), Standard & Poor's and Barclays Capital Index Products to compare mutual fund investor returns to an appropriate set of benchmarks.
There are actually three primary causes for the chronic shortfall for both equity and fixed income investors:
    1. Capital not available to invest. This accounts for 25 percent to 35 percent of the shortfall.
    2. Capital needed for other purposes. This accounts for 35 percent to 45 percent of the shortfall.
    3. Psychological factors. These account for 45 percent to 55 percent of the shortfall."

The key findings of Dalbar's QAIB report provide compelling statistics about how individual investment strategies produced negative outcomes for the majority of investors:

- Psychological factors account for 45 percent to 55 percent of the chronic investment return shortfall for both equity and fixed income investors.
- Asset allocation is designed to handle the investment decision-making for the investor, which can materially reduce the shortfall due to psychological factors.
- Successful asset allocation investing requires investors to act on two critical imperatives:
  1. Balance capital preservation and appreciation so that they are aligned with the investor's objective.
  2. Select a qualified allocator.
- The best way for an investor to determine their risk tolerance is to utilize a risk tolerance assessment. However, these assessments must be accessible and usable.
- Evaluating allocator quality requires analysis of the allocator's underlying investments, decision making process and whether or not past efforts have produced successful outcomes.

- Choosing a top allocator makes a significant difference in the investment results one will achieve.
- Mutual fund retention rates suggest that the average investor has not remained invested for long enough periods to derive the potential benefits of the investment markets.
- Retention rates for asset allocation funds exceed those of equity and fixed income funds by over a year.
- Investors' ability to correctly time the market is highly dependent on the direction of the market. Investors generally guess right more often in up markets. However, in 2012 investors guessed right only 42 percent of the time during a bull market.
- Analysis of investor fund flows compared to market performance further supports the argument that investors are unsuccessful at timing the market. Market upswings rarely coincide with mutual fund inflows while market downturns do not coincide with mutual fund outflows.
- Average equity mutual fund investors gained 15.56 percent compared to a gain of 15.98 percent that just holding the S&P 500 produced.
- The shortfall in the long-term annualized return of the average mutual fund equity investor and the S&P 500 continued to decrease in 2012.
- The fixed-income investor experienced a return of 4.68 percent compared to an advance of 4.21 percent on the Barclays Aggregate Bond Index.
- The average fixed income investor has failed to keep up with inflation in nine out of the last 14 years.*

It doesn't take a financial services market research report to tell you that market volatility is out of your control. The report does prove,

---

2013 QAIB, Dalbar, March 2013

however, that before you experience market volatility, you should have an investment plan, and when the market is fluctuating, you should stand by your investment plan. You should also review and discuss your investment plan with your financial professional on a regular basis, ensuring he/she is aware of any changes in your goals, financial circumstances, your health or your risk tolerance. When the economy is under stress and the markets are volatile, investors can feel vulnerable. That vulnerability causes people to tinker with their portfolios in an attempt to outsmart the market. Financial professionals, however, don't try to time the market for their clients. They try to tap into the gains that can be realized by committing to long-term investment strategies.

CHAPTER 6 CALL TO ACTION //

- Beware the danger zone when making withdrawals on a market investment without principal guarantees. If the account suffers a loss, rapid depletion of your funds will change what the future of your retirement looks like. The timing of market downturns is more critical to retirees than to the average investor.

- Do the math of rebounds to understand the realities of market loss. You have to do more than just earn back your initial loss in order to get back to where you were before. Use the percentage of the investment and not dollar amount to calculate what you need to earn in order to recapture your losses.

- Realize that your emotions inevitably enter the mix during stock market downturns. According to the DALBAR "Quantitative Analysis of Investment Behavior" report released in 2013, the average fixed income investor managing their money alone failed to keep up with inflation in nine out of the last 14 years.

- Visit the SHM Financial website (shmfinancial.com) to view the Financial Overview Part II video. Financial professionals don't try to outsmart the market when managing investments for their clients. Instead, they tap into the potential for gains by committing to proven and long-term investment strategies.

7

WHAT IS MANAGED MONEY?

Philip is 69 years old. He retired four years ago. He relied on income from an IRA for three years in order to increase his Social Security benefit. He also made significant investments in 36 different mutual funds. He chose to diversify among the funds by selecting a portion for growth, another for good dividends, another that focused on promising small cap companies and a final portion that work like index funds. All the money that Philip had in mutual funds he considered Need Later Money that he wanted to rely on in his 80s. After the stock market took a hit in 2008, Philip lost some confidence in his investments and decided to sit down with us to see if his portfolio was able to recover.

We were able to determine what goals he had in mind. Specifically, we determined what Philip actually wanted and needed the money for, and when he needed it. We also looked inside each of the mutual funds and discovered several instances of overlap. While Philip had created diversity in his portfolio by selecting funds focused on different goals, he didn't account for overlap in the companies in which the funds were invested. Out of the 36 funds, we found that 20 owned nearly identical stocks. While most of the companies were good investments, the high instance of overlap did not contribute to the healthy investment diversity that Philip wanted. We also provided him with a report that explained the concentration ratio of his holdings (noting how much of his portfolio was contained within the top 25 stock holdings), the percentage of his portfolio that each company in which he invested represented (showing the percentage of net assets that each company made up as an overall position in his portfolio) and the portfolio date of his account (showing when the funds in his portfolio were last updated: as funds are required to report updates only twice per year, it was possible that some of his fund reports could be six months old).

We consolidated his assets into one investment management strategy. This allowed Philip's investments to be managed by someone he trusted who knew his specific investment goals and needs. Eliminating redundancy and overlap in his portfolio was easy to do but difficult to detect since Philip had multiple funds with multiple brokerage firms. Philip sat down with us to see if his mutual funds could perform well, and he left with a consolidated management plan and a money manager that understood him personally. That's Managed Money at its best.

Now that you've calculated the Rule of 110, determined how much risk you have and how much you want (if any), and you've determined how much Green Money you need to meet your short-term and mid-term income needs, it's time to look at what you have left. The money you have left after you've calculated your income needs has the potential of becoming Red Money:

your stocks, mutual funds and other investment instruments that you want to continue accumulating value with the market. You now have the luxury of taking a closer second look at your Red, Hope So Money to determine how you would like to manage it.

As you read earlier in the key findings of the DALBAR report, the deck is stacked against the individual investor. Remember that the average investor on a fixed income failed to keep pace with inflation in nine of the last 14 years, meaning the inherent risk in managing your Red Money is very real and could have a lasting impact on your assets. So, how much of your Red Money do you invest, and in what kinds of markets, investment products and stocks do you invest? There are a lot of different directions in which you can take your Red Money. One thing is for sure: significant accumulation depends on investing in the market. How you go about doing it is different for everyone. Gathering stocks, bonds and investment funds together in a portfolio without a cohesive strategy behind them could cause you to miss out on the benefits of a more thoughtful and planful approach. The end result is that you may never really understand what your money is doing, where and how it is really invested, and which investment principles are behind the investment products you hold. While you may have goals for each individual piece of your portfolio, it is likely that you don't have a comprehensive plan for your Red Money, which may mean that *you are taking on more risk than you would like, and are getting less return for it than is possible.*

Enter *Managed Money.* **Managed Money is money that is managed by a professional *with a purpose.*** After your income needs are met and you have assets that you would like to dedicate to accumulation, there are decisions you need to make about how to invest those assets. You can buy stocks, index funds, mutual funds, bonds—you name it—you can invest in it. However, the difference between Red Money and Managed Money is that Managed Money has a cohesive strategy behind it that is *implemented* *by a professional.* When you manage your Red Money with an investment plan, it becomes Managed Money: *money that is being managed with a specific purpose, a specific set of focused goals and a specific strategy in mind.* Managed Money is still a type of Hope So Money and it comes with different levels of risk. But Managed Money is under the watchful eye of professionals who have a stake in the success of your money in the market and who can recommend a range of strategies from those designed for preservation to those targeting rapid growth. You don't want to miss out on achieving the right level of risk, and more importantly, composing a careful plan for the return of your assets.

It can be helpful to think of Red Money and Managed Money using this analogy:

If you needed to travel through an unfamiliar city in a foreign country, you could rent a car or perhaps hire a driver. Were you to drive yourself, you would try to gain guidance from perplexing road signs and need to adhere to traffic rules—with no experience or assistance to lean on. It would take longer to get to where you want to go, and the chance of a traffic accident would be higher. If you hired a driver, they would manage your journey. A driver would know the route, how to avoid traffic, and follow the rules of the road.

Red Money is like driving yourself. With Managed Money, you are still traveling by car, but now you have a professional working on your behalf.

TAKING A CLOSER LOOK AT YOUR PORTFOLIO

Think about your investment portfolio. Think specifically of what you would consider your Red Money. Do you know what is there? You may have several different investment products like individual mutual funds, bond accounts, stocks, and alternative investments. You may have inherited a stock portfolio from a relative, or you might be invested in a bond account offered by the company for which you worked due to your familiarity with them. While you may or may not be managing your investments individually, the reality is that you probably don't have an overall management strategy for all of your investments. Investments that aren't managed are simply Red Money, or money that is at risk in the market.

Harnessing the earning potential of your Red Money relies on more than a collection of stocks and bonds, however. It needs guided management. A good money manager uses the knowledge they have about the level of risk with which you are comfortable, what you need or want to use your money for, when you want or need it and how you want to use it. The Managed Money investments that they choose for you will still have a certain level of risk, but under the right management, control and process, you have a far better chance of a successful outcome that meets your specific needs.

When you sit down with an investment professional, you can look at all of your assets together. Chances are that you have accumulated a number of different assets over the last 20, 30 or 50 years. You may have a 401(k), an IRA, a Roth IRA, an account of self-directed stocks, a brokerage account, etc. Wherever you put your money, a financial professional will go through your assets and help you determine the level of risk to which you are exposed now and should be exposed in the future.

AVOIDING EMOTIONAL INVESTING

There's no way around it; people get emotional about their money. And for good reason. You've spent your life working for it, exchanging your time and talent for it, and making decisions about how to invest it, save it and make it grow. The maintenance of your lifestyle and your plans for retirement all depend on it. The best investment strategies, however, don't rely on emotions. One of Managed Money's greatest strengths lies in the fact that it is managed by someone who understands your needs and desires, but doesn't make decisions about your money under the influence of emotion.

A well-managed investment account meets your goals as a whole, not in individualized and piecemeal ways. Professional money managers do this by creating requirements for each type of investment in which they put your money. We'll call them "screens." Your money manager will run your holdings through the screens they have created to evaluate different types of investment strategies. A professionally managed account will only have holdings that meet the requirements laid out in the overall management plan that was designed to meet your investment goals. The holdings that don't make it through the screens, the ones that don't contribute to your investment goals, are sold and redistributed to investments that your financial professional has determined to be appropriate.

Different screens apply to different Managed Money strategies. For example, if one of your goals is significant growth, which would require taking on more risk alongside the potential for more return, an investment professional would screen for companies that have high rates of revenue and sales growth, high earnings growth, rising profit margins, and innovative products. On the other hand, if you want your portfolio to be used for income, which would call for lower risk and less return, your professional would screen for dividend yield and sector diversification. *Every investor has a different goal, and every goal requires a customized strategy that uses quantitative screens.* A professional will create a portfolio that reflects your investment desires. If some of the current assets you own complement the strategies that your professional recommends, those will likely stay in your portfolio.

Screening your assets removes emotions from the equation. It removes attachment to underperforming or overly risky investments. Financial professionals aren't married to particular stocks or mutual funds for any reason. They go by the numbers and see your portfolio through a lens shaped by your retirement goals. Your professional understands your wants and needs, and creates an investment strategy that takes your life events and future plans into account. It's a planful approach, and it allows you to tap into the tools and resources of a professional who has built a career around successful investing. Managing money is a full-time job and is best left to a professional money manager.

Removing emotions from investing also allows you to be unaffected by the day-to-day volatility of the market. Your financial professional doesn't ask where the market is going to be in a year, three years or a month from now. If you look at the value of the stock market from the beginning of the twentieth century to today, it's going up. Despite the Great Depression, despite the 1987 crash, despite the 2008 market downturn, the market, as a whole, trends up. Remember the major market downturn in 2008 when the market lost 30 percent of its value? Not only did it completely recover, it has far exceeded its 2008 value. Emotional investing led countless people to sell low as the market went down, and buy the same shares back when the market started to recover. That's an expensive way to do business. While you can't afford to lose money that you need in two, three or five years, your Need Later Money has time to grow. One way to do so is to make it Managed Money.

CREATING AN INVESTMENT STRATEGY

Just like Philip in our previous story example, chances are that you can benefit from taking a more managed investment approach tailored to your goals. Managed Money is generally Need Later Money that you want to grow for needs you'll have in at least 10 years. You can work with your financial planner to create investments that meet your needs within different timeframes. You may need to rely on some of your Managed Money in 10, 15 or 20 years, whether for additional income, a large purchase you plan on making or a vacation. Whatever you want it for, you will need it down the road. A financial professional can help you rescale the risk of your assets as they grow, helping you lock in your profits and secure a source of income you can depend on later.

So what does a Managed Money account look like? Here's what it *doesn't* look like: a portfolio with 49 small cap mutual funds, a dozen individual stocks and an assortment of bond accounts. A brokerage account with a hodgepodge of investments, even if goal-oriented, is not a professionally managed account. It's still Red Money. Remember, Managed Money is an account overseen by a professional that has an overarching investment philosophy. When you look at making investments that will perform to meet your future income needs, the burning question becomes: How much should you have in the market and how should it be invested? Working with a professional will help you determine how much risk you should take, how to balance your assets so they will meet your goals and how to plan for the big ticket items, like health care expenses, that may be in your future. Yes, Managed Money is exposed to risk, but by working with a professional, you can manage that risk in a productive way.

WHY MANAGED MONEY?

If you have met your immediate income needs for retirement, why bother with professionally managing your other assets? The money you have accumulated above and beyond your income needs probably has a greater purpose. It may be for your children or grandchildren. You may want to give money to a charity or organization that you admire. In short, you may want to craft your legacy. It would be advantageous to grow your assets in the best manner possible. A financial professional has built a career around managing money in profitable ways. They are experts under the supervision of the organization that they represent.

Turning to Managed Money also means that you don't have to burden yourself with the time commitment, the stress, and the cost of determining how to manage your money. Managed Money can help you better enjoy your retirement. Do you want to sit down in your home office every day and determine how to best allocate your assets, or do you want to be living your life while someone else manages your money for you? When the majority of your Red Money is managed with a specific purpose by a financial professional, you don't have to be worrying about which stocks to buy and sell today or tomorrow.

SEEKING FINANCIAL ADVICE: STOCK BROKERS VS. A REGISTERED INVESTMENT ADVISOR (RIA)

Investors basically have access to two types of advice in today's financial world: advice from stock brokers and advice given by investment advisors. Most investors, however, don't know the difference between types of advice and the people from whom they receive advice. Today, there are two primary types of advice offered to investors: advice given by a commission-based registered representative (brokers) and advice given by fee-based Registered Investment Advisors. Unfortunately, many investors are not aware that a difference exists; nor have they been explained the distinction between the two types of advice. In a survey taken by TD Ameritrade, the top reasons investors choose to work with an independent registered investment advisor are:*

- Registered Investment Advisors are required, as fiduciaries, to offer advice that is in the best interest of clients
- More personalized service and competitive fee structure offered at a Registered Investment Advisor firm
- Dissatisfaction with full commission brokers

---

* *2011 Advisor Sentiment Study, commissioned by TD AMERITRADE. TD Ameritrade, Inc.*

The truth is that there is a great deal of difference between stock brokers and Registered Investment Advisors. For starters, Registered Investment Advisors are obligated to act in an investor's best interests in every aspect of a financial relationship. Confusion continues to exist among investors struggling to find the best financial advice out there and the most credible sources of advice.

Here is some information to help clear up the confusion so you can find good advice from a professional you can trust:

- Registered Investment Advisors have the fiduciary duty to act in a client's best interest at all times with every investment decision they make. Stock brokers and brokerage firms usually do not act as fiduciaries to their investors and are not obligated to make decisions that are entirely in the best interest of their customers. For example, if you decide you want to invest in precious metals, a stock broker would offer you a precious metals account from their firm. An Registered Investment Advisor would find you a precious metals account that is the best fit for you based on the investment strategy of your portfolio.

- Registered Investment Advisors give their clients a Form ADV describing the methods that the professional uses to do business. A Registered Investment Advisor also obtains client consent regarding any conflicts of interest that could exist with the business of the professional.

- Stock brokers and brokerage firms are not obligated to provide comparable types of disclosure to their customers.

- Whereas stock brokers and firms routinely earn large profits by trading as principal with customers, Registered Investment Advisors cannot trade with clients as principal (except in very limited and specific circumstances).

- Registered Investment Advisors charge a pre-negotiated fee with their clients in advance of any transactions. They cannot earn additional profits or commissions from their customers' investments without prior consent. Registered Investment Advisors are commonly paid an asset-based fee that aligns their interests with those of their clients. Brokerage firms and stock brokers, on the other hand, have much different payment agreements. Their revenues may increase regardless of the performance of their customers' assets.

- Unlike brokerage firms, where investment banking and underwriting are commonplace, Registered Investment Advisors must manage money in the best interests of their customers. Because Registered Investment Advisors charge set fees for their services, their focus is on their client. Brokerage firms may focus on other aspects of the firm that do not contribute to the improvement of their clients' assets.
- Unlike brokers, Registered Investment Advisors do not get commissions from fund or insurance companies for selling their investment products.

Just to drive home the point, here is what a fiduciary duty to a client means for a Registered Investment Advisor. Registered Investment Advisors must:*

- Always act in the best interest of their client and make investment decisions that reflect their goals.
- Identify and monitor securities that are illiquid.
- When appropriate, employ fair market valuation procedures.
- Observe procedures regarding the allocation of investment opportunities, including new issues and the aggregation of orders.

---

* *2011 Advisor Sentiment Study, commissioned by TD AMERITRADE. TD Ameritrade, Inc.*

- Have policies regarding affiliated broker-dealers and maintenance of brokerage accounts.
- Disclose all conflicts of interest.
- Have policies on the use of brokerage commissions for research.
- Have policies regarding directed brokerage, including step-out trades and payment for order flow.
- Abide by a code of ethics.

CHAPTER 7 CALL TO ACTION //

- Ask your financial professional if a Managed Money portfolio is a good option for your goals, objectives and risk tolerance. Managed Money is managed by a professional with a purpose. It is still considered a type of Red Money, but there is a dedicated direction, strategy and end goal in mind, which makes it less dangerous.
- Imagine that Red Money is like driving yourself in unfamiliar territory. With Managed Money, you are still traveling by car, but now you have a professional driving on your behalf.
- Call 1-800-MONEY-SHM (1-800-666-3974) for a specific overview of your current portfolio to see if a managed money option might be right for you.

8

NEW IDEAS FOR
INVESTING

What if I need to access my money?

Beau is a corn and soybean farmer with 1,200 acres of land. He routinely retains somewhere between $40,000 and $80,000 in his checking and savings accounts. If a major piece of equipment fails and needs repair or replacement, Beau will need the money available to pay for the equipment and carry on with farming. If the price of feed for his cattle goes up one year, he will need to compensate for the increased overhead to his farming operation. He isn't a particularly wealthy farmer, but he has little choice but to keep a portion of money on hand in case something comes up and he must access it quickly. Most of his capital is held in livestock in the pasture or crops in the ground tied up for six to eight months of the year. When a major financial need arises, Beau can't just harvest 10 acres of soybeans and *use them for payment. He needs to depend heavily on Liquidity in order to be a successful farmer.*

Old habits die hard, however, and when Beau finally hangs up his overalls and quits farming, he keeps his bank accounts flush with cash, just like in the old days. After selling the farm and the equipment, Beau keeps a huge portion of the profits in liquid investments because that's what he is familiar with. Unfortunately for Beau, with his pile of money sitting in his checking account, he isn't even keeping pace with inflation. After all his hard work as a farmer, his money is losing value every day because he didn't shift to a paradigm of leveraging his assets to generate income and accumulate value.

Almost anything would be a better option for Beau than clinging to Liquidity. When you essentially keep your money under the mattress, you don't keep up with inflation. He could have done something better to get either more return from his money or more safety, and at the very least would not have lost out to inflation.

WHAT IS YOUR EXIT STRATEGY?

Throughout the book, we have discussed how investment options require advice that is relevant to today. Traditional, outdated investment strategies are not only ineffective; they can be harmful to the average investor. One of the most traditional ways of thinking about investing is the risk versus reward trade-off. It goes something like this:

Investment options that are considered safer carry less risk, but also offer the potential for less return. Riskier investment options carry the burden of volatility and a greater potential for loss, but they also offer a greater potential for large rewards. Most professionals move their clients back and forth along this range, shifting between investments that are safer and investments that are structured for growth. Essentially, the old rules of investing dictate that you can either choose relative safety *or* return, but you can't have both.

Finding a solution to the liquidity/safety/return dilemma is an important part of income planning because people are living longer now than they used to. The longer we live, the more changes we see. Your portfolio must be flexible enough to adapt to these changes, allowing you access to your money when you need it. Updated investment strategies work with the flexibility of liquidity to provide exit strategies and remake the rules. Here is how:

There are three dimensions that are inherent in any investment: *Liquidity, Safety,* and *Return*. You can maximize any two of these dimensions at the expense of the third. If you choose Safety and Liquidity, this is like keeping your assets in a checking account or savings account. This option delivers a lot of Safety and Liquidity, but at the expense of any Return. On the other hand, if you choose Liquidity and Return, meaning you have the potential for great return and can still reclaim your money whenever you choose, you will likely be exposed to a very high level of risk.

Understanding Liquidity can help you break the old Risk versus Safety trade-off. By identifying assets from which you don't require Liquidity, you can place yourself in a position to potentially profit from relatively safe investments that provide a higher than average rate of return.

Choosing Safety and Return over Liquidity can have significant impacts on the accumulation of your assets. In the example story of Beau and his liquid investment portfolio, the paradigm shift from earning and saving to leveraging assets was a costly one. The sooner you want your money back, the less you can leverage it for Safety or Return. If you have the option of putting your money in a long-term investment, you will be sacrificing Liquidity, but potentially gaining both Safety and Return. Rethinking your approach to money in this way can make a world of difference and can provide you with a structured way to generate income while allowing the value of your assets to grow over time.

YOUR EMERGENCY FUND

Working with your financial planner to customize an income plan with an emergency fund built in is one way to strengthen the balance of liquidity, safety and return within your portfolio. Having a bucket designated as the emergency fund means you won't have to worry about exiting from a series of investments in order to access your money. When the unexpected happens, if your son or daughter need financial assistance or the heat or air conditioning unit blows out or the engine falls out of your car, you know what bucket of money you can safely dip into without triggering a tax event or other unintended consequences.

Liquidity is the most essential component of an emergency fund, because you want to be able to access this money quickly and easily. These are funds you can get to within 30 days or less. This money also has to be safe, because you will need to know this money is there in the event of an emergency. Going back to having the right tool for the right job, your emergency fund will ideally be placed in a safe, Know So Money investment tool such as a money market account or a short term CD at your local bank.

How much do you need to have in your emergency fund? The amount of an emergency fund can vary. Four to six months of income is a commonly used amount, but there can be legitimate reasons why that amount could be more or less.

The question is, how much Liquidity do you *really* need? Think about it. If you haven't sat down and created an income plan for your retirement, your perceived need for Liquidity is a guess. You don't know how much cash you'll need to fill the income gap if you don't know the amount of your Social Security benefit of the total of your other income options. If you *have* determined your income need and have made a plan for filling your income gap, you can partition your assets based on when you will need them. With an income plan in place, *you can use new rules to enjoy both Safety and Return from your assets.*

CHAPTER 8 CALL TO ACTION //

- The three aspects of any investment include liquidity, safety, and return. You can choose to maximize any two against the third.
- Choosing to maximize liquidity alone can be an expensive option because the sooner you need your money back, the less you can leverage it for safety and return. To plan for a successful retirement in today's economy requires a creative use of today's financial tools.
- A comprehensive income plan during retirement should include provisions for an emergency fund. This fund should be a liquid account you can readily access. **The ideal tool for an emergency fund is a bank savings account or short term CD.**

9

TAKING ADVANTAGE OF
TAX STRATEGIES

*You make more money by saving on taxes
than you do by making more money.*

Everyone is familiar with taxes (you've been paying them your entire working life), but not everyone is familiar with how to make tax planning a part of their retirement strategy. There is nothing wrong with maximizing the tax deferral and tax advantage type strategies that are available. This is especially true during retirement when you are no longer bringing new money into your asset base from an income or earning point of view. During retirement, you are in the positon of having to create an income flow from the assets that are already there. ***During this phase in your life, keeping more of your money is on par with earning***

more money. You have to take advantage of all the different tax planning strategies that are at your disposal.

Tax planning and ***tax reporting*** are two very different things. Most people only *report* their taxes. March rolls around, people pull out their 1040s or use TurboTax to enter their income and taxable assets, and ship it off to Uncle Sam at the IRS. If you use a CPA to report your taxes, you are essentially paying them to record history. You have the option of being proactive with your taxes and to plan for your future by making smart, informed decisions about how taxes affect your overall financial plan. Working with a financial professional who, along with a CPA, makes recommendations about your finances to you, will keep you looking forward instead of in the rearview mirror as you enter retirement.

TAX PLANNING DURING YOUR RETIREMENT YEARS

When you retire, you move from the earning and accumulation phase of your life into the asset distribution phase of your life. For most people, that means relying on Social Security, a 401(k), an IRA, or a pension. Wherever you have put your Green Money for retirement, you are going to start relying on it to provide you with the income that once came as a paycheck. Most of these distributions will be considered income by the IRS and will be taxed as such. There are exceptions to that (not all of your Social Security income is taxed, and income from Roth IRAs is not taxed), but for the most part, your distributions will be subject to income taxes.

Regarding assets that you have in an old 401(k) or an IRA plan, when you reach 70 ½ years of age, you will be required to draw a certain amount of money from your retirement asset as income each year. That amount depends on your age and the balance in your IRA. The amount that you are required to withdraw as income is called a Required Minimum Distribution (RMD). Why are you required to withdraw money from your own account? Chances are the money in that account has grown over time, and the government wants to collect taxes on that growth. If you have a large balance in an IRA, there's a chance your RMD could increase your income significantly enough to put you into a higher tax bracket, subjecting you to a higher tax rate.

Here's where tax planning can really begin to work strongly in your favor. In the distribution phase of your life, you have a predictable income based on your RMDs, your Social Security benefit and any other income-generating assets you may have. What really impacts you at this stage is how much of that money you keep in your pocket after taxes. Essentially, *you will make more money saving on taxes than you will by making more money.* If you can reduce your tax burden by 30, 20 or even 10 percent, you earn yourself that much more money by not paying it in taxes.

How do you save money on taxes? By having a plan. In this instance, a financial professional can work with the CPAs at their firm to create a **distribution plan** that minimizes your taxes and maximizes your annual net income.

BUILDING A TAX DIVERSIFIED PORTFOLIO

So far so good: avoid taxes, maximize your net annual income and have a plan for doing it. When people decide to leverage the experience and resources of a financial professional, they may not be thinking of how distribution planning and tax planning will benefit their portfolios. Taxes, however, play a crucial role in retirement planning. Achieving those tax goals requires knowledge of tax laws, foresight and professional guidance.

Finding the path to a good tax plan isn't always a simple task. Every tax return you file is different from the one before it because things constantly change. Your expenses change. Planned or unplanned purchases occur. Health care costs, medical bills, an inheritance, property purchases, reaching an age where your

RMD kicks in or travel, any number of things can affect how much income you report and how many deductions you take each year.

Preparing for the ever-changing landscape of your financial life requires a tax-diversified portfolio that can be leveraged to balance the incomes, expenditures and deductions that affect you each year. A financial professional will work with you to answer questions like these:

- What does your tax landscape look like?
- Do you have a tax-diversified portfolio robust enough to adapt to your needs?
- Do you have a diversity of taxable and non-taxable income planned for your retirement?
- Will you be able to maximize your distributions to take advantage of your deductions when you retire?
- Is your portfolio strong enough and tax-diversified enough to adapt to an ever-changing (and usually increasing) tax code?

» *When Molly returns home after a week in the hospital recovering from a knee replacement, the 77-year-old calls her daughter, sister and brother to let them know she is home and feeling well. She also should have called her CPA. Molly's medical expenses for the procedure, her hospital stay, her medications and the ongoing physical therapy she attended amount to more than $50,000.*

*Currently, Americans can deduct medical expenses that are more than 7.5 percent of their Adjusted Gross Income (AGI). Molly's AGI is $60,000 the year of her knee replacement, meaning she is able to deduct $44,000 of her medical bills from her taxes that year. Her AGI dictated that she could deduct more than 80 percent of her medical expenses that year. **Molly didn't know this.***

Had she been working with a financial professional who regularly asked her about any changes in her life, her spending, or her expenses (expected or unexpected), Molly could have saved thousands of dollars. Molly can also file an amendment to her tax return to recoup the overpayment.

This relatively simple example of how tax planning can save you money is just the tip of the iceberg. No one can be expected to know the entire U.S. tax code. But a professional who is working with a team of CPAs and financial professionals have an advantage over the average taxpayer who must start from square one on their own every year. Have you been taking advantage of all the deductions that are available to you?

PROACTIVE TAX PLANNING

The implications of proactive tax planning are far reaching, and are larger than many people realize. Remember, doing your taxes in January, February, March or April means you are writing a history book. Planning your taxes in October, November or December means that you are writing the story as it happens. You can look at all the factors that are at play and make decisions that will impact your tax return *before* you file it.

Realizing that tax planning is an aspect of financial planning is an important leap to make. When you incorporate tax planning into your financial planning strategy, it becomes part of the way you maximize your financial potential. Paying less in taxes means you keep more of your money. Simply put, the more money you keep, the more of it you can leverage as an asset. This kind of planning can affect you at any stage of your life. If you are 40 years old, are you contributing the maximum amount to your 401(k) plan? Are you contributing to a Roth IRA? Are you finding ways to structure the savings you are dedicating to your children's education? Do you have life insurance? Taxes and tax planning affects all of these investment tools. Having a relationship with a professional who works with a CPA can help you build a truly comprehensive financial plan that not only works with your investments, but also shapes your assets to find the most efficient ways to prepare for tax time. There may be years that you could benefit from higher distributions because of the tax bracket that you are in, or there could be years you would benefit from taking less. There may be years when you have a lot of deductions and years you have relatively few. **Adapting your distributions to work in concert with your available deductions** is at the heart of smart tax planning. Professional guidance can bring you to the next level of income distribution, allowing you to remain flexible enough to maximize your tax efficiency. And remember, saving money on taxes makes you more money than making money does.

What you have on paper is important: your assets, savings, investments, which are financial expression of your work and time. It's just as important to know how to get it off the paper in a way that keeps most of it in your pocket. Almost anything that involves financial planning also involves taxes. Annuities, investments, IRAs, 401(k)s, 403(b), and many other investment options will have tax implications. Life also has a way of throwing curveballs. Illness, expensive car repair or replacement, or *any event that has a financial impact on your life will likely have a corresponding tax implication* around which you should adapt your financial plan. Tax planning does just that.

One dollar can end up being less than 25 cents to your heirs.

» *When Joe's father passed away, he discovered that he was the beneficiary of his father's $500,000 IRA. Joe has a wife and a family of four children, and he knew that his father had intended for a large portion of the IRA to go toward funding their college educations.*

After Joe's father's estate is distributed, Joe, who is 50 years old and whose two oldest sons are entering college, liquidates the IRA. By doing so, his taxable income for that year puts him in a 39.6 percent tax bracket, immediately reducing the value of the asset to $302,000. An additional 3.8 percent surtax on net investment income further diminishes the funds to $283,000. Liquidating the IRA in effect subjects much of Joe's regular income to the surtax, as well. At this point, Joe will be taxed at 43.4 percent.

Joe's state taxes are an additional 9 percent. Moreover, estate taxes on Joe's father's assets claim another 22 percent. By the time the IRS is through, Joe's income from the IRA will be taxed at 75 percent, leaving him with $125,000 of the original $500,000. While it would help contribute to the education of his children, it wouldn't come anywhere near completely paying for it, something the $500,000 could have easily done.

As the above example makes clear, leaving an asset to your beneficiaries can be more complicated than it may seem. In the case of a traditional IRA, after federal, estate and state taxes, the asset could literally diminish to as little as 25 percent of its value.

How does working with a professional help you make smarter tax decisions with your own finances? Any financial professional worth their salt will be working with a firm that has a team of trained tax professionals, including CPAs, who have an intimate knowledge of the tax code and how to adapt a financial plan to it.

Here's another example of how taxes have major implications on asset management:

» Greg and Rhonda, a 62-year-old couple, begin working with a financial professional in October. After structuring their assets to reflect their risk tolerance and creating assets that

would provide them Green Money income during retirement, they feel good about their situation. They make decisions that allow them to maximize their Social Security benefits, they have plenty of options for filling their income gap, and have begun a safe yet ambitious Managed Money strategy with their professional. When their professional asks them about their tax plan, they tell him their CPA handled their taxes every year, and did a great job. Their professional says, "I don't mean who does your taxes, I mean, who does your tax planning?" Greg and Rhonda aren't sure how to respond.

Their professional brings Greg and Rhonda's financial plan to the firm's CPA and has her run a tax projection for them. A week later their professional calls them with a tax plan for the year that will save them more than $3,000 on their tax return. The couple is shocked. A simple piece of advice from the CPA based on the numbers revealed that if they paid their estimated taxes before the end of the year, they would be able to itemize it as a deduction, allowing them to save thousands of dollars.

This solution won't work for everyone, and it may not work for Greg and Rhonda every year. That's not the point. By being proactive with their approach to taxes and using the resources made available by their financial professional, they were able to create a tax plan that saved them money.

MANAGED MONEY AND TAXES

There are also tax implications for the money that you have managed professionally. People with portions of their investment portfolio that are actively traded can particularly benefit from having a proactive tax strategy. Without going into too much detail, for tax purposes there are two kinds of investment money: qualified and non-qualified. Different investment strategies can have different effects on how you are taxed on your investments and the growth of your investments. Some are more beneficial for one kind of investment strategy over another. Determining how to plan for the taxation of non-qualified and qualified investments is fodder for holiday party discussions at accounting firms. While it may not be a stimulating topic for the average investor, you don't have to understand exactly how it works in order to benefit from it.

While there are many differences between qualified and non-qualified investments, the main difference is this: qualified plans are designed to give investors tax benefits by deferring taxation of their growth until they are withdrawn. Non-qualified investments are not eligible for these deferral benefits. As such, non-qualified investments are taxed whenever income is realized from them in the form of growth.

Actively and non-actively traded investments provide a simple example of how to position your investments for the best tax advantage. In an actively traded and managed portfolio, there is a high amount of buying and selling of stocks, bonds, funds, ETFs, etc. If that active portfolio of non-qualified investments does well and makes a 20 percent return one year and you are in the 39.6 percent tax bracket, your net gain from that portfolio is only about 12 percent (39.6 percent tax of the 20 percent gain is roughly 8 percent.) In a passive trading strategy, you can use a qualified investment tool, such as an IRA, to achieve 13, 14 or 15 percent growth (much lower than the actively traded portfolio), but still realize a higher net return because the growth of the qualified investment is not taxed until it is withdrawn.

Does this mean that you have to always rely on a buy and hold strategy in qualified investment tools? Not necessarily. The question is, if you have qualified and non-qualified investments, where do you want to position your actively traded and managed assets? Incorporating a planful approach to positioning your investments for more beneficial taxation can be done many ways, but let's consider one example. Keeping your actively managed investment strategies inside an IRA or some other qualified plan could allow you to realize the higher gains of those investments without paying tax on their growth every year. Your more passively managed funds could then be kept in taxable, non-qualified vehicles and methods, and because you aren't realizing income from them on an annual basis by frequently trading them, they grow sheltered from taxation.

If you are interested in taking advantage of tax strategies that maximize your net income, you need the attentive strategies, experience and knowledge of a professional who can give you options that position you for profit. At the end of the day, what's important to you as the consumer is how much you keep, your after-tax take home.

WHAT IS ESTATE ARBITRAGE?

Although we have two chapters of this book devoted to legacy planning, it bears mentioning here that if you have an RMD birthday coming up and you don't need the funds, it might make sense to look at more tax efficient options that could preserve more of your legacy. One such option is something we called Estate Arbitrage.

Consider the following scenario: if you have $400,000 in an IRA, and your heirs take the money as a lump sum distribution, the amount is reduced due to tax obligations to between $200,000 and $300,000. What we do with estate arbitrage is to take the required RMD on the IRA to buy a life insurance policy. This policy has the potential to give your heirs $400,000 of tax free legacy value depending on their age and health. Some life insurance instruments also have long term care riders attached to them as well, so you can help to solve that problem, also.

If you have to take the money out of your IRA anyway, and if you don't need the income, estate arbitrage can be an extremely tax efficient manner in which to create a legacy and pass money on to your beneficiaries. Think of it as a way to take a portion of your money and pass it on to your heirs without having to share any with Uncle Sam. Each case is different based on health and age. For further information and to see if you qualify, call the number listed at the end of the chapter.

We also make use of a "combination program" which takes advantage of a guaranteed stream of payment from your IRA paid out over 3-10 years to fund a TAX FREE guaranteed benefit made available to your heirs.

ESTATE TAXES

The government doesn't just tax your income from investments while you're alive. They will also dip into your legacy.

While estate taxes aren't as hot of a topic as they were a few years ago, they are still an issue of concern for many people with assets. While taxes may not apply on estates that are less than $5 million, certain states have estate taxes with much lower exclusion ratios. Some are as low as $600,000. Many people may have to pay a state estate tax. One strategy for avoiding those types of taxes is to move assets outside of your estate. That can include gifting them to family or friends, or putting them into an irrevocable trust. Life insurance is another option for protecting your legacy. In addition to the Federal estate tax, each state has its own state inheritance tax. Make sure you are aware of what your current state inheritance tax is.

CHAPTER 9 CALL TO ACTION //

- Plan your taxes with a financial professional to proactively find the best options for your tax return. Knowing how to use tax law in your favor means putting more money in your wallet and less money into the hands of Uncle Sam.

- Understand the tax repercussions when tapping into assets from a 401(k) or a traditional IRA for use an income source. Money that is considered qualified by the Federal government must be taxed upon distribution.

- Mark you RMD birthday on the calendar. At the age of 70 ½, the Federal Government requires all IRA participants to take their RMD, or Required Minimum Distribution. Failure to take your RMD can cost you thousands of dollars in taxes and penalty fees.

- Meet regularly with your financial professional to keep abreast of how tax law changes affect your financial plan.

- Call 1-800-MONEY-SHM (1-800-666-3974) to find out if Estate Arbitrage makes sense in your situation. Estate Arbitrage is one way to begin building a tax-free legacy for your heirs using the RMD money from your IRA.

10

PROTECTING YOUR ASSETS FROM FUTURE TAX CHANGES

What are the chances that my taxes will go up?

As the political winds change, it's critical to the health of anyone's retirement plan to meet regularly with an advisory team to both keep abreast and take advantage of all the tax rules and changes as they take place. The one thing we know for sure is that things will definitely change. Having various exit strategies in place will give you the ability to do different things at different times, keeping more of your money in your wallet and less in the hands of Uncle Sam.

THE FUTURE OF U.S. TAXATION

The raising of the debt ceiling raised more than just the ability for our government to go further into debt. It also raised concerns and fears about the future of our economy. Unfortunately, the general public is in a no-win situation for this solution to the problem. Printing money does not bode well for economic growth. This creates inflationary pressures that devalue the U.S. dollar and make everyone less wealthy. Cutting the entitlements that compose this liability leaves millions of people without benefits they have come to expect. The only other option, and one that the government knows all too well, is increasing taxes. In fact, according to a Congressional Budget Office paper issued in 2004:

"The term 'unfunded liability' has been used to refer to a gap between the government's projected financial commitment under a particular program and the revenues that are expected to be available to fund that commitment. But no government obligation can be truly considered 'unfunded' because of the U.S. government's sovereign power to tax—which is the ultimate resource to meet its obligations."

A balanced budget will be required at some point and with this will come higher taxes. We have uncertainty surrounding tax rates and how high they will go. Whether it is only on the top earners or unilaterally across all income levels is yet to be seen, but an increase of some sort will most certainly occur.

How do you prepare? Why spend so much time reassuring you that taxes will increase? Because you have an opportunity to take action. Now is the time to prepare for what will come and structure countermeasures for the good, the bad and the ugly of each of these legislative nightmares through tax-advantaged retirement planning.

You make more money by saving on taxes than you do by making more money. The simplistic logic of the statement makes sense when you discover it takes $1.50 in earnings to put that same dollar, saved in taxes, back in your pocket.

We spend our whole lives saving and accumulating wealth but spend so little time determining how to distribute this accumulation so as to retain it. Proactively planning for taxes is one way to make sure we have the appropriate diversification of taxable versus non-taxable assets to complement our distribution strategy.

THE BENEFITS OF DIVERSIFICATION

Heading into retirement, we should be situated with a diversified tax landscape. The point to spending our whole lives accumulating wealth is not to see the size of the number on paper, but rather to be an exercise in how much we put in our pocket after removing it from the paper. To truly understand tax diversification, we must understand what types of money exist and how each of these will be treated during accumulation and, most importantly, during distribution. The following is a brief summary:

1. Free money
2. Tax-advantaged money
3. Tax-deferred money
4. Taxable money
   a. Ordinary income
   b. Capital gains and qualified dividends

FREE MONEY

Free money is the best kind of money regardless of tax treatment because, in the end, you have more money than you would have otherwise. Many employers will provide contributions toward employee retirement accounts to offer additional employment benefits and encourage employees to save for their own retirement. With this, employers often will offer a matching contribution in which they contribute up to a certain percentage of an employee's salary (generally three to five percent) toward that employee's retirement account when the employee contributes to their retirement account as well. For example, if an employee earns $50,000 annually and contributes three percent ($1,500) to their retirement account annually, the employer will also contribute three percent ($1,500) to the employee's account. That is $1,500 in free money. Take all you can get! Bear in mind that any employer contribution to a 401(k) will still be subject to taxation when withdrawn.

TAX-ADVANTAGED MONEY

Tax-advantaged money is the next best thing to free money. Although you have to earn tax-advantaged money, you do not have to give part of it away to Uncle Sam. Tax-advantaged money comes in three basic forms that you can utilize during your lifetime; four if prison inspires your future, but we are not going to discuss that option.

One of the most commonly known forms of tax-advantaged money is municipal bonds, which earn and pay interest that could be tax-advantaged on the federal level, or state level, or both. There are several caveats that should be discussed with regard to the notion of tax-advantaged income from municipal bonds. First, you will notice that tax-advantaged has several flavors from the state and federal perspective. This is because states will generally tax the interest earned on a municipal bond unless the bond is offered from an entity located within that state. This severely limits the availability of completely tax-advantaged municipal bonds and constrains underlying risk and liquidity factors. Second, municipal bond interest is added back into the equation for determining your modified adjusted gross income (MAGI) for Social Security. This could push your income above a threshold and subject a portion of your Social Security income to taxation.

In effect, if this interest subjects some other income to taxation then this interest is truly being taxed.

Last, municipal bond interest may be excluded from the regular federal tax system, but it is included for determining tax under the alternative minimum tax (AMT) system. In its basic form, the AMT system is a separate tax system that applies if the tax computed under AMT exceeds the tax computed under the regular tax system. The difference between these two computations is the alternative minimum tax.

TAX-ADVANTAGED MONEY: ROTH IRA

Roth accounts are probably the single greatest tax asset that has come from Congress outside of life insurance. They are well known but rarely used. Roth IRAs were first established by the Taxpayer Relief Act of 1997 and named after Senator William Roth, the chief sponsor of the legislation. Roth accounts are simply an account in the form of an individual retirement account or an employer sponsored retirement account that allows for tax-advantaged growth of earnings and, thus, tax-advantaged income.

The main difference between a Roth and a traditional IRA or employer-sponsored plan lies in the timing of the taxation. We are all very familiar with the typical scenario of putting money away for retirement through an employer plan, whereby they deduct money from our paychecks and put it directly into a retirement account. This money is taken out before taxes are calculated, meaning we do not pay tax on those earnings today. A Roth account, on the other hand, takes the money after the taxes have been removed and puts it into the retirement account, so we do pay tax on the money today. The other significant difference between these two is taxation during distribution in later years. Regarding our traditional retirement accounts, when we take the money out later it is added to our ordinary income and is taxed accordingly. Additionally, including this in our income subjects us to the consequences mentioned above for municipal bonds with Social Security taxation, AMT, as well as higher Medicare premiums. A Roth on the other hand is distributed tax-advantaged and does not contribute toward negative impact items such as

Social Security taxation, AMT, or Medicare premium increases. It essentially comes back to us without tax and other obligations.

The best way to view the difference between the two accounts is to look at the life of a farmer. A farmer will buy seed, plant it in the ground, grow the crops and harvest it later for sale. Typically, the farmer would only pay tax on the crops that have been harvested and sold. But if you were the farmer, would you rather pay tax on the $5,000 of seed that you plant today or the $50,000 of crops harvested later? The obvious answer is $5,000 of seed today. The truth to the matter is that you are a farmer, except you plant dollars into your retirement account instead of seeds into the earth.

So why doesn't everyone have a Roth retirement account if things are so simple? There are several reasons, but the single greatest reason has been the constraints on contributions. If you earned over certain thresholds (MAGI over $125,000 single and $183,000 joint for 2012), you were not eligible to make contributions, and until last year, if your modified adjusted gross income (MAGI) was over $100,000 (single or joint), you could not convert a traditional IRA to a Roth. Outside these contribution limits, most people save for retirement through their employers and most employers do not offer Roth options in their plans. The reason behind this is because Roth accounts are not that well understood and people have been educated to believe that saving on taxes today is the best possible course of action.

TAX-ADVANTAGED MONEY: LIFE INSURANCE

As previously mentioned, the single greatest tax asset that has come from Congress outside of life insurance is the Roth account. Life insurance is the little-known or little-discussed tax asset that holds some of the greatest value in your financial history both during life and upon death. It is by far the best tax-advantaged device available. We traditionally view life insurance as a way to protect our loved ones from financial ruin upon our demise and it should be noted that everyone who cares about someone should have life insurance. Purchasing a life insurance policy ensures that our loved ones will receive income from the life insurance company to help them pay our final expenses and carry on with their lives without us comfortably when we die. The best part of the life insurance windfall is the fact that nobody will have to pay tax on the money received. This is the single greatest tax-advantaged device available, but it has one downside, we do not get to use it. Only our heirs will.

The little known and discussed part of life insurance is the cash value build-up within whole life and universal life (permanent) policies. Life insurance is not typically seen as an investment vehicle for building wealth and retirement planning, although we should discuss briefly why this thought process should be re-evaluated. Permanent life insurance is generally misconceived as something that is very expensive for a wealth accumulation vehicle because there are mortality charges (fees for the death benefit) that detract from the available returns. Furthermore, those returns do not yield as much as the stock market over the long run. This is why many times you will hear the phrase "buy term and invest the rest," where "term" refers to term insurance.

Let us take a second to review two terms just used in regard to life insurance: term and permanent. Term insurance is an idea with which most people are familiar. You purchase a certain death benefit that will go to your heirs upon death and this policy will be in effect for a certain number of years, typically 10 to 20 years. The 10 to 20 years is the term of the policy and once you have reached that end you no longer have insurance unless you purchase another policy.

Permanent insurance on the other hand has no term involved. It is permanent as long as the premiums continue to be paid. Permanent insurance generally initially has higher premiums than term insurance for the same amount of death benefit coverage and it is this difference that is referred to when people say "invest the rest."

Simply speaking there are significant differences between these two policies that are not often considered when providing a comparative analysis of the numbers. One item that gets lost in the fray when comparing term and permanent insurance is that term usually expires before death. In fact, insurance studies show less than one percent of all term policies pay out death benefit claims. The issue arises when the term expires and the desire to have more insurance is still present.

A term policy with the same benefit will be much more expensive than the original policy and, many times, life events occur, such as cancer or heart conditions, which makes it impossible to acquire another policy and leaves your loved ones unprotected and tax-advantaged legacy planning out of the equation.

Another aspect and probably the most important piece in consideration of the future of taxation is the fact that permanent insurance has a cash accumulation value. Two aspects stand out with the cash accumulation value. First, as the cash accumulation value increases the death benefit will also increase whereas term insurance remains level. Second, this cash accumulation offers value to you during your lifetime rather than to your heirs upon death. The cash accumulation value can be used for tax-advantaged income during your lifetime through policy loans. Most importantly, this tax-advantaged income is available during retirement for distribution planning, all while offering the same typical financial protection to your heirs.

TAX-DEFERRED MONEY

Tax-deferred money is the type of money with which most of people are familiar, but we also briefly reviewed the idea above. Tax-deferred money is typically our traditional IRA, employer sponsored retirement plan or a non-qualified annuity. Essentially, you put money into an investment vehicle that will accumulate in value over time and you do not pay taxes on the earnings that grow these accounts until you distribute them. Once the money is distributed, taxes must be paid. However, the same negative consequences exist with regard to additional taxation and expense in other areas as previously discussed. The cash accumulation value can be used for tax-advantaged income.

TAXABLE MONEY

Taxable money is everything else and is taxable today, later or whenever it is received. These four types of money come down to two distinct classifications: taxable and tax-free. The greatest difference when comparing taxable and tax-advantaged income is a function of how much money we keep after tax. For help in determining what the differences should be, excluding outside factors such as Social Security taxation and AMT, a tax equivalent yield should be used.

TAX-ADVANTAGED IN THE REAL WORLD

To put the tax equivalent yield into perspective, let us look at an example: Bob and Mary are currently retired, living on Social Security and interest from investments and falling within the 25 percent tax bracket. They have a substantial portion of their investments in municipal bonds yielding 6 percent, which is quite comforting in today's market. The tax equivalent yield they would need to earn from a taxable investment would be 8 percent, a 2 percent gap that seems almost impossible given current market volatility. However, something that has never been put into perspective is that the interest from their municipal bonds is subject to taxation on their Social Security benefits (at 21.25 percent). With this, the yield on their municipal bonds would be 4.725

percent, and the taxable equivalent yield falls to 6.3 percent, leaving a gap of only 1.575 percent.

In the end, most people spend their lives accumulating wealth through the best, if not the only vehicle they know, a tax-deferred account. This account is most likely a 401(k) or 403(b) plan offered through our employer and may be supplemented with an IRA that was established at one point or another. As the years go by, people blindly throw money into these accounts in an effort to save for a retirement that we someday hope to reach.

The truth is, most people have an age selected for when they would like to retire, but spend their lives wondering if they will ever be able to actually quit working. To answer this question, you must understand how much money you will have available to contribute toward your needs. *In other words, you need to know what your after-tax income will be during this period.*

All else being equal, it would not matter if you put your money into a taxable, tax-deferred or tax-advantaged account as long as income tax rates never change and outside factors are never an event. The net amount you receive in the end will be the same.

Unfortunately, this will never be the case. We already know that taxes will increase in the future, meaning we will likely see higher taxes in retirement than during our peak earning years.

Regardless, saving for retirement in any form is a good thing as it appears from all practical perspectives that future government benefits will be cut and taxes will increase. You have the ability to plan today for efficient tax diversification and maximization of our after-tax dollars during your distribution years.

CHAPTER 10 CALL TO ACTION //

- Count on the trend of increasing taxation. The future of U.S. taxation is uncertain but change is always certain. A closer examination of the debt ceiling and taxes throughout U.S. history points to the benefits and necessity of tax diversification.

- Take action now to prepare for the rise in taxes by restructuring your assets to include the benefits of free and tax-advantaged money. Tax-advantaged money is money you earn without having to pay taxes on. One of the most common forms includes municipal bonds, but be aware these come with many state and federal caveats and complexities.

- Understand that Roth IRAs and life insurance are two forms of tax-advantaged money that can take advantage of today's lower tax rate when preparing for tomorrow's retirement.

- Schedule a Tax Preparation Review to have your taxes reviewed by a national CPA firm to see if there are mistakes being made that are costing you unnecessary money. Call 1-800-MONEY-SHM (1-800-666-3974) to schedule your review today.

11

ADVANTAGES AND DISADVANTAGES OF THE ROTH CONVERSION

To convert, or not to convert. That is the question.

Louis Brandeis provides one of the best examples illustrating how tax planning works. Brandeis was Associate Justice on the Supreme Court of the United States from 1916 to 1939. Born in Louisville, Kentucky, Brandeis was an intelligent man with a touch of country charm. He described tax planning this way:

"I live in Alexandria, Virginia. Near the Court Chambers, there is a toll bridge across the Potomac. When in a rush, I pay the dollar toll and get home early. However, I usually drive outside the downtown section of the city and cross the Potomac on a free bridge.

The bridge was placed outside the downtown Washington, D.C. area to serve a useful social service—getting drivers to drive the extra mile and help alleviate congestion during the rush hour.

If I went over the toll bridge and through the barrier without paying a toll, I would be committing tax evasion.

If I drive the extra mile and drive outside the city of Washington to the free bridge, I am using a legitimate, logical and suitable method of tax avoidance, and I am performing a useful social service by doing so.

*The tragedy is that **few people know that the free bridge exists.**"*

Like Brandeis, most American taxpayers have options when it comes to "crossing the Potomac," so to speak. It's a financial planner's job to tell you what options are available. You can wait until March to file your taxes, at which time you might pay someone to report and pay the government a larger portion of your income. However, you could instead file before the end of the year, work with your financial professional and incorporate a tax plan as part of your overall financial planning strategy. Filing later is like crossing the toll bridge. Tax planning is like crossing the free bridge.

Which would you rather do?

The answer to this question is easy. Most people want to save money and pay less in taxes. What makes this situation really difficult in real life, however, is that the signs along the side of the road that direct us to the free bridge are not that clear. To normal Americans, and to plenty of people who have studied it, the U.S. tax code is easy to get lost in. There are all kinds of rules, exceptions to rules, caveats and conditions that are difficult to understand, or even to know about. What you really need to know is your options and the bottom line impacts of those options.

ROTH IRA CONVERSIONS

The attractive qualities of Roth IRAs may have prompted you to explore the possibility of moving some of your assets into a Roth account. Another important difference between the accounts is how they treat Required Minimum Distributions (RMDs). When you turn 70 ½ years old, you are required to take a minimum amount of money out of a traditional IRA. This amount is your RMD. It is treated as taxable income. Roth IRAs, however, do not have RMDs, and their distributions are not taxable. Quite a deal, right?

While having a Roth IRA as part of your portfolio is a good idea, converting assets to a Roth IRA can pose some challenges, depending on what kinds of assets you want to transfer. The success of your conversion will all depend on the timing.

You may have heard about converting your IRA to a Roth IRA, but you might not know the full net result on your income. The main difference between the two accounts is that the growth of investments within a traditional IRA is not taxed until income is withdrawn from the account, whereas taxes are charged on contribution amounts to a Roth IRA, not withdrawals. The problem, however, is that when assets are removed from a traditional IRA, even if the assets are being transferred to a Roth IRA account, taxes apply.

There are a lot of reasons to look at Roth conversions. People have a lot of money in IRAs, up to multiple millions of dollars. Even with $500,000, when they turn 70 ½ years old, their RMD is going to be approximately $18,000, and they have to take that out whether they want to or not. It's a tax issue. Essentially, if you will be subject to high RMDs, it could have impacts on how much of your Social Security is taxable, and on your tax bracket.

By paying taxes now instead of later on assets in a Roth IRA, you can realize tax-advantaged growth. You pay once and you're done paying. Your heirs are done paying. It's a powerful tool. Here's a simple example to show you how powerful it can be:

Imagine that you pay to convert a traditional IRA to a Roth. You have decided that you want to put the money in a vehicle that gives you a tax-advantaged income option down the road. If you pay a 25 percent tax on that conversion and the Roth IRA then doubles in value over the next 10 years, you could look at your situation as only having paid 12.5 percent tax.

The prospect of tax-advantaged income is a tempting one. While you have to pay a conversion tax to transfer your assets, you also have turned taxable income into tax free retirement money that you can let grow as long as you want without being required to withdraw it.

There are options, however, that address this problem. Much like the Brandeis story, there may be a "free bridge" option for many investors.

Your financial professional will likely tell you that it is not a matter of whether or not you should perform a Roth IRA conversion, it is a matter of how much you should convert and when.

Here are some of the things to consider before converting to a Roth IRA:

- If you make a conversion before you retire, you may end up paying higher taxes on the conversion because it is likely that you are in some of your highest earning years, placing you in the highest tax bracket of your life. It is possible that a better strategy would be to wait until after you retire, a time when you may have less taxable income, which would place you in a lower tax bracket.

- Many people opt to reduce their work hours from fulltime to part-time in the years before they retire. If you have pursued this option, your income will likely be lower, in turn lowering your tax rate.

- The first years that you draw Social Security benefits can also be years of lower reported income, making it another good time frame in which to convert to a Roth IRA.

One key strategy to handling a Roth IRA conversion is to ***always be able to pay the cost of the tax conversion with outside money***. Structuring your tax year to include something like a significant deduction can help you offset the conversion tax. This way you aren't forced to take the money you need for taxes from the value of the IRA. The reason taxes apply to this maneuver is because when you withdraw money from a traditional IRA, it is treated as taxable income by the IRS. Your financial professional, with the help of the CPAs at their firm, may be able to provide you with options like after-tax money, itemized deductions or other situations that can pose effective tax avoidance options.

Some examples of avoiding Roth IRA conversions taxes include:

- *Using medical expenses that are above 10 percent of your Adjusted Gross Income.* If you have health care costs that you can list as itemized deductions, you can convert an amount of income from a traditional IRA to a Roth IRA that is offset by the deductible amount. Essentially, deductible medical expenses negate the taxes resulting from recording the conversion.
- *Individuals, usually small business owners, who are dealing with a Net Operating Loss (NOL).* If you have NOLs, but aren't able to utilize all of them on your tax return, you can carry them forward to offset the taxable income from the taxes on income you convert to a Roth IRA.
- *Charitable giving.* If you are charitably inclined, you can use the amount of your donations to reduce the amount of taxable income you have during that year. By matching the amount you convert to a Roth IRA to the amount

your taxable income was reduced by charitable giving, you can essentially avoid taxation on the conversion. You may decide to double your donations to a charity in one year, giving them two years' worth of donations in order to offset the Roth IRA conversion tax on this year's tax return.

- *Investments that are subject to depletion.* Certain investments can kick off depletion expenses. If you make an investment and are subject to depletion expenses, they can be deducted and used to offset a Roth IRA conversion tax.

Not all of the above scenarios work for everyone, and there are many other options for offsetting conversion taxes. The point is that you have options, and your financial professional and tax professional can help you understand those options.

If you have a traditional IRA, Roth conversions are something you should look at. As you approach retirement you should consider your options and make choices that keep more of your money in your pocket, not the government's.

ADDITIONAL TAX BENEFITS OF ROTH IRAS

Not only do Roth IRAs provide you with tax-advantaged growth, they also give you a tax diversified landscape that allows you to maximize your distributions. Chances are that no matter the circumstances, you will have taxed income and other assets subject to taxation. *But if you have a Roth IRA, you have the unique ability to manage your Adjusted Gross Income (AGI), because you have a tax-advantaged income option!*

Converting to a Roth IRA can also help you preserve and build your legacy. Because Roth IRAs are exempt from RMDs, after you make a conversion from a traditional IRA, your Roth account can grow tax-advantaged for another 15, 20 or 25 years and it can be used as tax-advantaged income by your heirs. It is important to note, however, that non-spousal beneficiaries do have to take RMDs from a Roth IRA, or choose to stretch it and draw tax-advantaged income out of it over their lifetime.

TO CONVERT OR NOT TO CONVERT?

Conversions aren't only for retirees. You can convert at any time. Your choice should be based on your individual circumstances and tax situation. Sticking with a traditional IRA or converting to a Roth, again, depends on your individual circumstances, including your income, your tax bracket and the amount of deductions you have each year. **A financial professional can analyze your specific situation and make a recommendation by running a Roth IRA Conversion Report.** This report breaks down the numbers to find out how long you would have to have the money in the Roth in order to overcome the tax expense of converting. It also breaks down from a tax point of view the level of income at which you don't want to exceed so you don't get put into a higher tax bracket.

Is it better to have a Roth IRA or traditional IRA? It depends on your individual circumstance. Some people don't mind having taxable income from an IRA. Their income might not be very high and their RMD might not bump their tax bracket up, so it's not as big a deal. A similar situation might involve income from Social Security. Social Security benefits are taxed based on other income you are drawing. If you are in a position where none or very little of your Social Security benefit is subject to taxes, paying income tax on your RMD may be very easy.

> » *There are also situations where leveraging taxable income from a traditional IRA can work to your advantage come tax time. For example, Grace and William dream of buying a boat when they retire. It is something they have looked forward to their entire marriage. In addition to the savings*

and investments that they created to supply them with income during retirement, which includes a traditional IRA, they have also saved money for the sole purpose of purchasing a boat once they stop working.

When the time comes and they finally buy the boat of their dreams, they pay an additional $15,000 in sales taxes that year because of the large purchase. Because they are retired and earning less money, the deductions they used to be able to realize from their income taxes are no longer there. The high amount of sales taxes they paid on the boat puts them in a position where they could benefit from taking taxable income from a traditional IRA.

When Grace and William's financial professional learns about their purchase, he immediately contacts a CPA at his firm to run the numbers. They determine that by taking a $15,000 distribution from their IRA, they could fulfill their income needs to offset the $15,000 sales tax deduction that they were claiming due to the purchase of their boat. In the end, they pay zero taxes on their income distribution from their IRA.

The moral of the story? ***Having a tax diversified landscape gives you options.*** Having capital assets that can be liquidated, tax-advantaged income options and sources that can create capital gains or capital losses will put you in a position to play your cards right no matter what you want to accomplish with your taxes. The ace up your sleeve is your financial professional and the CPAs they work with. Do yourself a favor and *plan* your taxes instead of *reporting* them!

CHAPTER 11 CALL TO ACTION //

- Look for the "free bridge" option in your tax strategy. Converting from a traditional to a Roth IRA can provide you with tax-advantaged retirement income.

- Be smart about a Roth IRA and find out if it makes sense to do a conversion to help you preserve and build your legacy.

- Schedule a **Roth IRA conversion Report** to find out how long you would have to have the money in your Roth in order to overcome the tax expense of converting. Call 1-800-MONEY-SHM (1-800-666-3974) and ask for more information about the Roth IRA Conversion Report.

12

YOUR LEGACY BEYOND DOLLARS AND CENTS

If you're like most people, planning your estate isn't on the top of your list of things to do. Planning your income needs for retirement, managing your assets and just living your life without worrying about how your estate will be handled when you are gone make legacy planning less than attractive for a Saturday afternoon task. The fact of the matter, however, is that if you don't plan your legacy, someone else will. That someone else is usually a combination of the IRS and other government entities: lawyers, executors, courts, and accountants. Who do you think has the best interests of your beneficiaries in mind?

Today, there is more consideration given to planning a legacy than just maximizing your estate. When most people think about an estate, it may seem like something only the very wealthy have: a stately manor or an enormous business. But a legacy is something else entirely. A legacy is more than the sum total of the financial assets you have accumulated. It is the lasting impression you make on those you leave behind. The dollar and cents are just a small part of a legacy.

A legacy encompasses the stories that others tell about you, shared experiences and values. An estate may pay for college tuition, but a legacy may inform your grandchildren about the importance of higher education and self-reliance.

A legacy may also contain family heirlooms or items of emotional significance. It may be a piece of art your great-grandmother painted, family photos, or a childhood keepsake.

Our goal is to make sure you are able to enjoy your own money as much as possible. Once we have achieved your financial security and independence, then we can talk about legacy. When you go about planning your legacy, certainly explore strategies that can maximize the financial benefit to the ones you care about. But also take the time to ensure that you have organized the whole of your legacy, and let that be a part of the last gift you leave.

Many people avoid planning their legacy until they feel they must. Something may change in your life, like the birth of a grandchild, the diagnosis of a serious health problem, or the death of a close friend or loved one. Waiting for tragedy to strike in order to get your affairs in order is not the best course of action. The emotional stress of that kind of situation can make it hard to make patient, thoughtful decisions. Taking the time to create a premeditated and thoughtful legacy plan will assure that your assets will be transferred where and when you want them when the time comes.

THE BENEFITS OF PLANNING YOUR LEGACY

The distribution of your assets, whether in the form of property, stocks, Individual Retirement Accounts, 401(k)s or liquid assets, can be a complicated undertaking if you haven't left clear instructions about how you want them handled. Not having a plan will cost more money and take more time, leaving your loved ones to wait (sometimes for years) and receive less of your legacy than if you had a clear plan.

Planning your legacy will help your assets be transferred with little delay and little confusion. Instead of leaving decisions about how to distribute your estate to your family, attorneys or financial professionals, preserve your legacy and your wishes by drafting a clear plan at an early age.

And while you know all that, it can still be hard to sit down and do it. It reminds you that life is short, and the relatively complicated nature of sorting through your assets can feel like a daunting task. But one thing is for sure: *it is impossible for your assets to be transferred or distributed the way you want at the end of your life if you don't have a plan.*

Ask yourself:

- Are my assets up to date?
- Have my primary and contingent beneficiaries been clearly designated?
- Does my plan allow for restriction of a beneficiary?
- Does my legacy plan address minor children that I want to provide with income?
- Does my legacy plan allow for multi-generational payout?

Answers to these questions are critical if you want the final say in how your assets are distributed. In order to achieve your legacy goals, you need a plan.

MAKING A PLAN

Eventually, when your income need is filled and you have sufficient standby money to meet your need for emergencies, travel or other extra expenses you are planning for, whatever isn't used during your lifetime becomes your financial legacy. The money that you do not use during your lifetime will either go to loved ones, unloved ones, charity, or the IRS. The questions is, who would you rather disinherit?

By having a legacy plan that clearly outlines your assets, your beneficiaries and your distribution goals, you can make sure that your money and property is ending up in the hands of the people you determine beforehand. Is it really that big of a deal? It absolutely is. Think about it. Without a clear plan, it is impossible for anyone to know if your beneficiary designations are current and reflect your wishes because you haven't clearly expressed who your beneficiaries are. You may have an idea of who you want your assets to go to, but without a plan, it is anyone's guess. It is also impossible to know if the titling of your assets is accurate unless you have gone through and determined whose name is on the titles. More importantly, *if you have not clearly and effectively communicated your desires regarding the planned distribution of your legacy, you and your family may end up losing a large part of it.*

As you can see, managing a legacy is more complicated than having an attorney read your will, divide your estate and write checks to your heirs. The additional issue of taxes, Family Maximum Benefit calculations and a host of other decisions rear their heads. Educating yourself about the best options for positioning your legacy assets is a challenging undertaking. Working with a financial professional who is versed in determining the most efficient and effective ways of preserving and distributing your legacy can save you time, money and strife.

So, how do you begin?

Making a Legacy Plan Starts with a Simple List. The first, and one of the largest, steps to setting up an estate plan with a financial professional that reflects your desires is creating a detailed inventory of your assets and debts (if you have any). You need to know what assets you have, who the beneficiaries are, how much they are worth and how they are titled. You can start by identifying and listing your assets. This is a good starting point for working with a financial professional who can then help you determine the detailed information about your assets that will dictate how they are distributed upon your death.

If you are particularly concerned about leaving your kids and grandkids a lifetime of income with minimal taxes, you will want to discuss a Stretch IRA option with your financial professional.

STRETCH IRAS: GETTING THE MOST OUT OF YOUR MONEY

In 1986, the U.S. Congress passed a law that allows for multi-generational distributions of IRA assets. This type of distribution is called a Stretch IRA because it stretches the distribution of the account out over a longer period of time to several beneficiaries. It also allows the account to continue accumulating value throughout your relatives' lifetimes. You can use a Stretch IRA as an income tool that distributes throughout your lifetime, your children's lifetimes and your grandchildren's lifetimes.

Stretch IRAs are an attractive option for those more concerned with creating income for their loved ones than leaving them with a lump sum that may be subject to a high tax rate. With traditional IRA distributions, non-spousal beneficiaries must generally take distributions from their inherited IRAs, whether transferred or not, within five years after the death of the IRA owner. An exception to this rule applies if the beneficiary elects to take distributions over his or her lifetime, which is referred to as stretching the IRA.

Let's begin by looking at the potential of stretching an IRA throughout multiple generations.

» *In this scenario, Mr. Cleaver has an IRA with a current balance of $350,000. If we assume a five percent annual rate of return, and a 28 percent tax rate, the Stretch IRA turned a $502,625 legacy into more than $1.5 million. Doubling the value of the IRA also provided Mr. Cleaver, his wife, two children and three grandchildren with income. Not choosing the stretch option would have cost nearly $800,000 and had impacts on six of Mr. Cleaver's loved ones.*

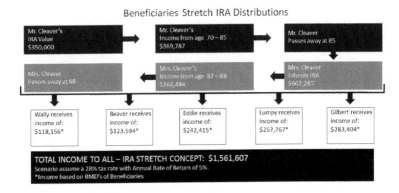

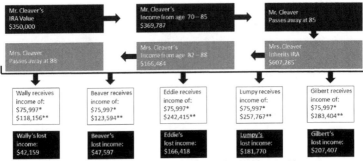

Unfortunately, many things may also play a role in failing to stretch IRA distributions. It can be tempting for a beneficiary to take a lump sum of money despite the tax consequences. Fortunately, if you want to solidify your plan for distribution, there are options that will allow you to open up an IRA and incorporate "spendthrift" clauses for your beneficiaries. This will ensure your legacy is stretched appropriately and to your specifications. Only certain insurance companies allow this option, and you will not find this benefit with any brokerage accounts. You need to work with a financial professional who has the appropriate relationship with an insurance company that provides this option.

CHAPTER 12 CALL TO ACTION //

- Consider the ways in which your legacy encompasses more than just the physical assets left behind for your children, grandchildren and charities or organizations. Your legacy is how you will be remembered.
- Educate yourself about the issues and complications that can complicate the management of a legacy.
- Work with a qualified financial professional to save you time, money and stress when it comes to the division of your estate.
- Begin your legacy planning by making a simple list.
- Visit the SHM Financial website (shmfinancial.com) to find out more about how you can begin your legacy planning.

13

PREPARING YOUR LEGACY:
WHAT CAN GO WRONG?

Jack organized his assets long ago. He started planning his retirement early and made investment decisions that would meet his needs. With a combination of IRA to Roth IRA conversions, a series of income annuities and a well-planned money management strategy overseen by his financial professional, he easily filled his income gap and was able to focus on ways to accumulate his wealth throughout his retirement. He reorganized his Know So and Hope So Money as he got older. When Jack retired, he had an income plan created that allowed him to maximize his Social Security benefit. He even had enough to accumulate wealth during his retirement. At this point, Jack turned his attention to planning his legacy. He wanted to know how he could maximize the amount of his legacy he will pass on to his heirs.

Jack met with an attorney to draw up a will, but he quickly learned that while having a will was a good plan, it wasn't the most efficient way to distribute his legacy. In fact, relying solely on a will created several roadblocks.

The two main problems that arose for Jack were *Probate* and *Unintentional Disinheritance:*

Problem #1: Probate

Probate. Just speaking the word out loud can cause shivers to run down your spine. Probate's ugly reputation is well deserved. It can be a costly, time consuming process that diminishes your estate and can delay the distribution of your estate to your loved ones. Nasty stuff, by any measure. Unless you have made a clear legacy plan and discussed options for avoiding probate, it is highly likely that you have many assets that might pass through probate needlessly. ***If your will and beneficiary designations aren't correctly structured, some of these assets will go through the probate process, which can turn dollars into cents.***

If you have a will, probate is usually just a formality. There is little risk that your will won't be executed per your instructions. The problem arises when the costs and lengthy timeline that probate creates come into play. Probate proceedings are notoriously expensive, lengthy and ponderous. A typical probate process identifies all of your assets and debts, pays any taxes and fees that you owe (including estate tax), pays court fees, and distributes your property and assets to your heirs. This process usually takes at least a year, and can take even longer before your heirs actually receive anything that you have left for them. For this reason, and because of the sometimes exorbitant fees that may be charged by lawyers and accountants during the process, probate has earned a nasty reputation.

Probate can also be a painstakingly public process. Because the probate process happens in court, the assets you own that go through a probate procedure become part of the public record. While this may not seem like a big deal to some, other people don't want that kind of intimate information available to the public.

Additionally, if your estate is entirely distributed via your will, the money that your family may need to cover the costs of your medical bills, funeral expenses and estate taxes will be tied up in probate, which can last up to a year or more. While immediate family members may have the option of requesting immediate cash from your assets during probate to cover immediate health care expenses, taxes, and fees, that process comes with its own set of complications. Choosing alternative methods for distributing your legacy can make life easier for your loved ones and can help them claim more of your estate in a more timely fashion than traditional methods.

A simpler and less tedious approach is to avoid probate altogether by structuring your estate to be distributed outside of the probate process. Two common ways of doing this are by structuring your assets inside a life insurance plan, and by using individual retirement planning tools like IRAs that give you the option of designating a beneficiary upon your death.

Problem #2: Unintentionally Disinheriting Your Family

You would never want to unintentionally disinherit a loved one or loved ones because of confusion surrounding your legacy plan. Unfortunately, it happens. Why? This terrible situation is typically caused by a simple lack of understanding. In particular, mistakes regarding legacy distribution occur with regards to those whom people care for the most: their grandchildren.

One of the most important ways to plan for the inheritance of your grandchildren is by properly structuring the distribution of your legacy. Specifically, you need to know if your legacy is going to be distributed *per stirpes* or *per capita*.

Per Stirpes. *Per stirpes* is a legal term in Latin that means "by the branch." Your estate will be distributed *per stirpes* if you designate each branch of your family to receive an equal share of your estate. In the event that your children predecease you, their share will be distributed evenly between their children—your grandchildren.

Per Capita. *Per capita* distribution is different in that you may designate different amounts of your estate to be distributed to members of the same generation.

Per stirpes distribution of assets will follow the family tree down the line as the predecessor beneficiaries pass away. On the other hand, per capita distribution of assets ends on the branch of the family tree with the death of a designated beneficiary. For example, when your child passes away, in a per capita distribution, your grandchildren would not receive distributions from the assets that you designated to your child.

What the terms mean is not nearly as important as what they do, however. The reality is that improperly titled assets could accidentally leave your grandchildren disinherited upon the death of their parents. It's easy to check, and it's even easier to fix.

A simple way to remember the difference between the two types of distribution goes something like this: "***Stirpes are forever and Capita is capped.***"

Another way to avoid complicated legacy distribution problems, and the probate process, is by leveraging a life insurance plan.

LIFE INSURANCE: AN IMPORTANT LEGACY TOOL

One of the most powerful legacy tools you can leverage is a good life insurance policy. Life insurance is a highly efficient legacy tool because it creates money when it is needed or desired the most.

Over the years, life insurance has become less expensive, while it offers more features, and it provides longer guarantees.

There are many unique benefits of life insurance that can help your beneficiaries get the most out of your legacy. Some of them include:

- Providing beneficiaries with a tax-free, liquid asset.
- Covering the costs associated with your death.
- Providing income for your dependents.
- Offering an investment opportunity for your beneficiaries.
- Covering expenses such as tuition or mortgage down payments for your children or grandchildren.

Very few people want life insurance, but nearly everyone wants what it does. Life insurance is specifically, and uniquely, capable of creating money when it is needed most. When a loved one passes, no amount of money can remove the pain of loss. And certainly, money doesn't solve the challenges that might arise with losing someone important.

It has been said that when you have money, you have options. When you don't have money, your options are severely limited. You might imagine a life insurance policy can give your family and loved ones options that would otherwise be impossible.

> » *Ron spent the last 20 years building a small business. In so many ways, it is a family business. Each of his three children, Maddie, Ruby and Edward, worked in the shop part-time during high school. But after all three attended college, only Maddie returned to join her father, and eventually will run the business full-time when Ron retires.*
>
> *Ron is able to retire comfortably on Social Security and on-going income from the shop, but the business is nearly his entire financial legacy. It is his wish that Maddie own the*

business outright, but he also wants to leave an equal legacy to each of his three children.

There is no simple way to divide the business into thirds and still leave the business intact for Maddie.

Ron ends up buying a life insurance policy to make up the difference. Ruby and Edward will receive their share of an inheritance in cash from the life insurance policy and Maddie will be able to inherit the business intact.

Ron is able to accomplish his goals, treat all three children equitably and leave Maddie the business she helped to build.

If you have a life insurance policy but you haven't looked at it in a while, you may not know how it operates, how much it is worth and how it will be distributed to your beneficiaries. You may also need to update your beneficiaries on your policy. In short, without a comprehensive review of your policy, you don't really know where the money will go or to whom it will go.

If you don't have a life insurance policy but are looking for options to maintain and grow your legacy, speaking with a professional can show you the benefits of life insurance. Many people don't consider buying a life insurance policy until some event in their life triggers it, like the loss of a loved one, an accident or a health condition.

BENEFITS OF LIFE INSURANCE

Life insurance is a useful and secure tool for contingency planning, ensuring that your dependents receive the assets that you want them to have, and for meeting the financial goals you have set for the future. While it bears the name "Life Insurance," it is, in reality, a diverse financial tool that can meet many needs. The main function of a life insurance policy is to provide financial assets for your survivors. Life insurance is particularly efficient at achieving this goal because it provides a tax-advantaged lump sum of money in the form of a death benefit to your beneficiary or beneficiaries. That financial asset can be used in a number of ways. It can be structured as an investment to provide income for your spouse or children, it can pay down debts, and it can be used to cover estate taxes and other costs associated with death.

Living Benefits:

Many of today's life insurance instruments have riders and provisions for increased income in the event of chronic illness. Often known as Living Benefits, these products provide you with the means to pay for home health care or a nursing home facility while you are still alive. With annuities, these benefits are sometimes known as "income doublers" because the fixed income contracted by the rider will double should you or your spouse require long term care. Even if it's too late to qualify for traditional long term care insurance, long term care riders on annuity and life insurance products might still be an option for you, and if you never need long term care, that money is not lost. Instead, your beneficiaries receive a legacy.

Tax Benefits:

Tax liabilities on the estate you leave behind are inevitable. Capital property, for instance, is taxed at its fair market value at the time of your death, unless that property is transferred to your spouse. If the property has appreciated during the time you owned it, taxation on capital gains will occur. Registered Retirement Savings Plans (RRSPs) and other similarly structured assets are also included as taxable income unless transferred to a beneficiary as well. Those are just a few examples of how an estate can become subject to a heavy tax burden. The unique benefits of a life insurance policy provide ways to handle this tax burden, solving any liquidity problems that may arise if your family members want to hold onto an illiquid asset, such as a piece of property or an investment. Life insurance can provide a significant amount of money to a family member or other beneficiary, and that money is likely to remain exempt from taxation or seizure.

Protection Benefits:
One of life insurance's most important benefits is that it is not considered part of the estate of the policy holder. The death benefit that is paid by the insurance company goes exclusively to the beneficiaries listed on the policy. This shields the proceeds of the policy from fees and costs that can reduce an estate, including probate proceedings, attorneys' fees and claims made by creditors. The distribution of your life insurance policy is also unaffected by delays of the estate's distribution, like probate. Your beneficiaries will get the proceeds of the policy in a timely fashion, regardless of how long it takes for the rest of your estate to be settled.

Investing a portion of your assets in a life insurance policy can also protect that portion of your estate from creditors. If you owe money to someone or some entity at the time of your death, a creditor is not able to claim any money from a life insurance policy or an annuity, for that matter. As an exception to this rule, if you had already used the life insurance policy as collateral against a loan. If a large portion of the money you want to dedicate to your legacy is sitting in a savings account, investment or other liquid form, creditors may be able to receive their claim on it before your beneficiaries get anything, that is if there's anything left. A life insurance policy protects your assets from creditors and ensures that your beneficiaries get the money that you intend them to have.

HOW MUCH LIFE INSURANCE DO YOU NEED?
Determining the type of policy and the amount right for you depends on an analysis of your needs. A financial professional can help you complete a needs analysis that will highlight the

amount of insurance that you require to meet your goals. This type of personalized review will allow you to determine ways to continue providing income for your spouse or any dependents you may have. A financial professional can also help you calculate the amount of income that your policy should replace to meet the needs of your beneficiaries and the duration of the distribution of that income.

You may also want to use your life insurance policy to meet any expenses associated with your death. These can include funeral costs, fees from probate and legal proceedings, and taxes. You may also want to dedicate a portion of your policy proceeds to help fund tuition or other expenses for your children or grandchildren. You can buy a policy and hope it covers all of those costs, or you can work with a professional who can calculate exactly how much insurance you need and how to structure it to meet your goals. Which would you rather do?

AVOIDING POTENTIAL SNAGS

There are benefits to having life insurance supersede the direction given in a will or other estate plan, but there are also some potential snags that you should address to meet your wishes. For example, if your will instructs that your assets be divided equally between your two children but your life insurance beneficiary is listed as just one of the children, the assets in the life insurance policy will only be distributed to the child listed as the beneficiary. The beneficiary designation of your life insurance supersedes your will's instruction. This is important to understand when designating beneficiaries on a policy you purchase. Work with a professional to make sure that your beneficiaries are accurately listed on your assets, especially your life insurance policies.

USING LIFE INSURANCE TO BUILD YOUR LEGACY

Depending on your goals, there are strategies you can use that could multiply how much you leave behind. Life insurance is one of the most surefire and efficient investment tools for building a substantial legacy that will meet your financial goals.

Here is a brief overview of how life insurance can boost your legacy:

- Life insurance provides an immediate increase in your legacy.
- It provides an income tax-advantaged death benefit for your beneficiaries.
- A good life insurance policy has the opportunity to accumulate value over time.
- It may have an option to include long-term care (LTC) or chronic illness benefits should you require them.

If your income needs for retirement are met, you may have extra assets that you want to earmark as legacy funds. By electing to invest those assets into a life insurance policy, you can immediately increase the amount of your legacy. Remember, **life insurance allows you to transfer a tax-advantaged lump sum of money to your beneficiaries. It remains in your control during your lifetime, can provide for your long-term care needs and bypasses probate costs.** And make no mistake, taxes can have a huge impact on your legacy. Not only that, income and assets from your legacy can have tax implications for your beneficiaries, as well.

Here's a brief overview of how taxes could affect your legacy and your beneficiaries:

- The higher your income, the higher the rate at which it is taxed.
- Withdrawals from qualified plans are taxed as income.

- What's more, when you leave a large qualified plan, it ends up being taxed at a high rate.
- If you left a $500,000 IRA to your child, they could end up owing as much as $140,000 in income taxes.
- However, if you could just withdraw $50,000 a year, the tax bill might only be $10,000 per year.

How could you use that annual amount to leave a larger legacy? Luckily, you can leverage a life insurance policy to avoid those tax penalties, preserving a larger amount of your legacy and freeing your beneficiaries from an added tax burden.

> » *When Isabella turned 70 years old, she decided it was time to look into life insurance policy options. She still feels young, but she remembers that her mother died in early 70s, and she wants to plan ahead so she can pass on some of her legacy to her grandchildren just like her grandmother did for her.*
>
> *Isabella doesn't really want to think about life insurance, but she does want the security, reliability and tax-advantaged distribution that it offers. She lives modestly, and her Social Security benefit meets most of her income needs. As the beneficiary of her late husband's Certificate of Deposit (CD), she has $100,000 in an account that she has never used and doesn't anticipate ever needing since her income needs were already met.*
>
> *After looking at several different investment options with a professional, Isabella decides that a Single Premium life insurance policy fits her needs best. She can buy the policy with a $100,000 one-time payment and she is guaranteed that it would provide more than the value of the contract to her beneficiaries. If she left the money in the CD, it would be subject to taxes. But for every dollar that she puts into the*

*life insurance policy, her beneficiaries are guaranteed at least that dollar plus a death benefit, and all of it will be **tax-free!** For $100,000, Isabella's particular policy offers a $170,000 death benefit distribution to her beneficiaries. By moving the $100,000 from a CD to a life insurance policy, Isabella increases her legacy by 70 percent. Not only that, she has also sheltered it from taxes, so her beneficiaries will be able to receive $1.70 for every $1.00 that she entered into the policy! While buying the policy doesn't allow her to use the money for herself, it does allow her family to benefit from her well-planned legacy.*

MAKE YOUR WISHES KNOWN

Estate taxes used to be a much hotter topic in the mid-2000s when the estate tax limits and exclusions were much smaller and taxed at a higher rate than today. In 2008, estates valued at $2 million or more were taxed at 45 percent. Just two years later, the limit was raised to $5 million dollars taxed at 35 percent. The limit has continued to rise ever since. The limit applies to fewer people than before. Estate organization, however, is just as important as ever, and it affects everyone.

Ask yourself:

- Are your assets actually titled and held the way you think they are?
- Are your beneficiaries set up the way you think they should be?
- Have there been changes to your family or those you desire as beneficiaries?

There is more to your legacy beyond your property, money, investments and other assets that you leave to family members, loved ones and charities. Everyone has a legacy beyond money. You also leave behind personal items of importance, your values and beliefs, your personal and family history, and your wishes. Beyond a will and a plan for your assets, it is important that you make your wishes known to someone for the rest of your personal legacy. When it comes time for your family and loved ones to make decisions after you are gone, knowing your wishes can help them make decisions that honor you and your legacy, and give meaning to what you leave behind. Your professional can help you organize.

Think about your:
- Personal stories / recollections
- Values
- Personal items of emotional significance
- Financial assets

Do you want to make a plan to pass these things on to your family?

WORKING WITH A PROFESSIONAL

Part of using life insurance to your greatest advantage is selecting the policy and provider that can best meet your goals. Venturing into the jungle of policies, brokers and salespeople can be over-whelming, and can leave you wondering if you've made the best decision. Working with a trusted financial professional can help you cut through the red tape, the "sales-speak" and confusion to find a policy that meets your goals and best serves your desires for your money. If you already have a policy, a financial profes-sional can help you review it and become familiar with the policy's premium, the guarantees the policy affords, its performance, and its features and benefits. A financial professional can also help you make any necessary changes to the policy.

> » *When Al turned 88, his daughter finally convinced him to meet with a financial professional to help him organize his assets and get a legacy in order. Although Al is reluctant to let*

a stranger in on his personal finances, he ends up very glad that he did.

In the process of listing Al's assets and beneficiaries, his professional finds a woman's name listed as the beneficiary of an old life insurance annuity that he owns. It turns out, the woman is Al's ex-wife who is still alive. Had Al passed away before his ex-wife, the annuities and any death benefits that came with them would have been passed on to his ex-spouse. This does not reflect his latest wishes.

Things change, relationships evolve and the way you would like your legacy organized needs to adapt to the changes that happen throughout your life. There may be a new child or grandchild in your family, or you may have been divorced or remarried. A professional will regularly review your legacy assets and ask you questions to make sure that everything is up to date and that the current organization reflects your current wishes.

CHAPTER 13 CALL TO ACTION //

- Look for an estate planning attorney to help you with your legacy planning needs. Legacy planning tools include the creation of wills, trusts, living wills, and durable power of attorney for health care considerations.
- Review your current life insurance policies in order to determine if refinancing your life insurance makes sense.
- Consider life insurance instruments as a financial tool that can provide the distribution of tax-free, liquid assets to your beneficiaries while significantly building your legacy. This tool can also provide Living Benefits to help you pay for the high costs of medical care while you are still living.
- Work with a financial professional to help you select the policy that best meets your needs. Call 1-800-MONEY-SHM (1-800-666-3974) to schedule a policy review.

14

CHOOSING A FINANCIAL PROFESSIONAL

How do you find someone you can trust?

From the moment you dip your toes into the retirement planning pool to the point you start swimming laps, your assets organized, your income needs met, and your accumulation and legacy plans in place, working with a professional that you trust can make all the difference in how well your retirement reflects your desires.

It is important to know what you are looking for before taking the plunge. There are many people that would love to handle your money, but not everyone is qualified to handle it in a way that leads to a holistic approach to creating a solid retirement plan.

The distinction being made here is that you should look for someone that puts your interests first and actively wants to help you meet your goals and objectives. Oftentimes, the products someone sells you matter less than their dedication to making sure that you have a plan that meets your needs.

Professionals take your whole financial position into consideration. They make plans that adjust your risk exposure, invest in tools that secure your desired income during retirement and create investment strategies that allow you to continue accumulating wealth during your retirement for you to use later or to contribute to your legacy. If you buy stocks with a broker, use a different agent for a life insurance policy and have an unmanaged 401(k) through your employer, working with a financial professional will consolidate the management of your assets so you have one trustworthy person quarterbacking all of the team elements of your portfolio. Financial products and investment tools change, but the concepts that lie behind wise retirement planning are lasting. In the end, a financial professional's approach is designed for those serious about planning for retirement. *Can you say the same thing about the person that advises you about your financial life?*

It's easy to see how choosing a financial professional can be one of the most important decisions you can make in your life. Not only do they provide you with advice, they also manage the personal assets that supply your retirement income and contribute to your legacy. So, how do you find a good one?

HOW TO FIND A FINANCIAL PROFESSIONAL YOU CAN TRUST

Taking care to select a financial professional is one of the best things you can do for yourself and for your future. Your professional has influence and control of your investment decisions, making their role in your life more than just important. Your financial security and the quality of your retirement depends on the decisions, investment strategies and asset structuring that you and your professional create.

Working with a professional is different than calling up a broker when you want to buy or trade some stock. This isn't a decision that you can hand off to anyone else. You need to bring your time and attention to the table when it comes to finding someone with whom you can entrust your financial life. Separating the wheat from the chaff will take some work, but you'll be happy you did it.

While no one can tell you exactly who to choose or how to choose them, the following information can help you narrow the field:

- You can start by asking your friends, family and colleagues for referrals. You will want to pay particular attention to the recommendations that you get from others who are in your similar financial situation and who have similar lifestyle choices. The professional for the CEO of your company may have a different skill-set than the skill-set of the professional befitting your cousin who has 3 kids and a Subaru like you. Do follow-up research on the Internet as well. Look up the people who have been recommended to you on websites like LinkedIn that show the work history, referrals and experience of the candidates that you find most attractive. You will also learn about the firms with or for whom they work. The investment philosophies and reputations of the companies they work for will tell you a lot about how they will handle your money.

- The other side of the coin, however, is that everyone and their brother has a recommendation about how you should manage your money and who should manage it for you. From hot stock tips to "the best money manager in the state," people love to share good information that makes them look like they are in-the-know. Nobody wants to talk about the bad stock purchases they made, the times they lost money and the poor selections they made regarding financial professionals or stock brokers.

If you decide to take a friend or family member's recommendation, make sure they have a substantial, long-term experience with the financial professional and that their glowing review isn't just based on a one-time "win."

- You can also use online tools like the search function of the Financial Planning Association (http://www.fpanet. org/) and the National Association of Personal Financial Advisors (http://www.napfa.org/). Most of the professionals listed on these sites do not earn commissions from selling financial products, but are instead paid on a fee-only basis for their services. It is important to understand how your professional is being paid. It is generally considered preferable to work with a fee-based professional who will not have conflicts of interests between earning a commission and acting in your best interests.

- Many professionals may also be brokers or dealers that can earn commissions on things like life insurance, certain types of annuities and disability insurance. These professionals have most likely intentionally overlapped their roles so that if their clients choose to purchase insurance or investment products that require a broker or dealer, those clients won't have to find an additional person to work with. Again, understanding the role of your professional will help you make your determination.

NARROWING THE FIELD

1. Decide on the Type of Professional with Whom You Want to Work. There are four basic kinds of financial professionals. Many professionals may play overlapping roles. It is important to know a professional's primary function, how they charge for their services and whether they are obligated to act in your best interest.

Registered representatives, better known as stockbrokers or bank / investment representatives, make their living by earning commissions on insurance products and investment services. Stockbrokers basically sell you things. The products from which they make the highest commission are sometimes the products that they recommend to their clients. If you want to make a simple transaction, such as buying or selling a particular stock, a registered representative can help you. Although registered representatives are licensed professionals, if you want to create a structured and planful approach to positioning your assets for retirement, you might want to consider continuing your search.

The term "planner" is often misused. It can refer to credible professionals that are CPAs, CFPs and ChFCs to your uncle's next door neighbor who claims to have a lead on some undervalued stock about to be "discovered." A wide array of people may claim to be planners because there are no requirements to be a planner. The term financial planner, however, refers to someone who is properly registered as an investment advisor and serves as a fiduciary as described below.

Financial professionals are the diamonds in the rough. These Registered Investment Advisors are compensated on a fee basis. They do, however, often have licensure as stockbrokers or insurance agents, allowing them to earn commissions on certain transactions. More importantly, **financial professionals are financial fiduciaries, meaning they are required to make financial decisions in your best interest and reflecting your risk tolerance.** Investment Advisors are held to high ethical standards and are highly regarded in the financial industry. Financial professionals also often take a more comprehensive approach to asset management. These professionals are trained and credentialed to plan and coordinate their clients' assets in order to meet their goals or retirement and legacy planning. They are not focused on individual stocks, investments or markets. They look at the big picture, the whole enchilada.

Money managers are on par with financial professionals. However, they are often given explicit permission to make investment decisions without advanced approval by their clients.

Understanding who you are working with and what their title is the first step to planning your retirement. While each of the above-mentioned types of financial professionals can help you with aspects of your finances, it is **financial professionals** who have the most intimate role, the most objective investment strategies and the most unbiased mode of compensation for their services. A financial professional can also help you with the non-financial aspects of your legacy and can help you find ways to create a tax planning strategy to help you save money.

2. Be Objective. At the end of the day, you need to separate the weak from the strong. While you might want a strong personal rapport with your professional, or you may want to choose your professional for their personality and positive attitude, it is more important that you find someone who will give sage advice regarding achieving your retirement goals.

It can be helpful to use a process of elimination to narrow the field of potential professionals. Look into five or six potential leads and cross off your list the ones that don't meet your requirements until only one or two remain. Cross-check your remaining choices against the list of things you need from a professional. Make sure they represent a firm that has the investment tools and products that you desire, and make sure they have experience in retirement planning. That is, after all, the main goal.

Don't be afraid to investigate each of your candidates. You'll want to ask the same questions and look for the same information from everyone you consider so you can then compare them and discern which is best for you. You'll want to take a look at the specific credentials of each professional, their experience and competence, their ethics and fiduciary status, their history and track record, and a list of the services that they offer. The professionals who meet all or most of your qualifications are the ones you will contact for an interview.

Potential professionals should meet your qualifications in the following categories:

- *Credentials:* Look at their experience, the quality of their education, any associations to which they belong and certifications they have earned. Someone who has continued their professional education through ongoing certifications will be more up-to-date on current financial practices compared to someone who got their degree 25 years ago and hasn't done a thing since.

- *Practices:* Look at the track record of your candidates, how they are compensated for their services, the reports and analysis they offer, and their value added services.

- *Services:* Your professional must meet your needs. If you are planning your retirement, you should work with someone who offers services that help you to that end. You want someone who can offer planning, advice on investment strategies, ways to calculate risk, advice on insurance and annuities products, and ways to manage your tax strategy.

- *Ethics:* You want to work with someone who is above board and does things the right way. Vet them by checking their compliance record, current licensing, fiduciary status and, yes, even their criminal record. You never know!

3. Ask for and Check References. Once you have selected two or three professionals that you want to meet, call or email them and ask for references. Every professional should be able to provide you with at least two or three names. In fact, they will probably be eager to share them with you. Most professionals rely on references for validation of their success, quality of services and likability. You should, however, take them with a grain of salt. You have no way to know whether or not references are a professional's friends or colleagues.

It is worth contacting references, however, to check for inconsistencies. Ask each reference the same set of questions to get the same basic information. How long have they been working with the professional? What kind of services have they used and were they happy with them? What type of financial planning did they use the professional for? Were they versed in the type of financial planning that you needed? You can also ask them direct questions to elicit candid responses. What was the full cost of the expenses that your professional charged you? Do the reports and statements you receive come from the same firm? Questions like these can help you get a sense of how well the reference knows their professional and whether or not they are a quality reference.

A good reference is a bit like icing on the cake. It's nice to have them, but nothing speaks louder than a good track record and quality experience. And remember that a good reference, while nice to hear, is relatively cheap. How many times have you heard someone on the golf course or at work telling you how great their stockbroker is? But how many times have you heard about the bad investments or losses they have experienced?

HOW TO INTERVIEW CANDIDATES

After vetting your candidates and narrowing down a list of professionals that you think might be a good fit for you, it's time to start interviewing.

When you meet in person with a professional, you want to take advantage of your time with them. The presentations and information that they share with you will be important to pay attention to, but you will also want to control some aspects of the interview. After a professional has told you what they want you to hear, it's time to ask your own questions to get the specific information you need to make your decision.

Make sure to prepare a list of questions and an informal agenda so that you can keep track of what you want to ask and what points you want the professional to touch on during the interview. Using the same questions and agenda will also allow you to more easily compare the professionals after you have interviewed them all. Remember that these interviews are just that, *interviews*. You are meeting with several professionals to determine with whom you want to work. Don't agree to anything or sign anything during an interview until after you have made your final decision.

It can also be helpful to put a time limit on your interviews and to meet the professionals at their offices. The time limit will keep things on track and will allow structured time for presentations and questions/discussion. By meeting them at their office, you can get a sense of the work environment, the staff culture and attitude, and how the firm does business. If you are unable to travel to a professional's office and must meet them at your home or office, make sure that your interviews are scheduled with plenty of time between so the professionals don't cross each other's paths.

You can use the following questions during an initial interview to get an understanding of how each professional does business and whether they are a good fit for you:

1. How do you charge for your services? How much do you charge? This information should be easy to find on their website, but if you don't see it, ask. Find out if they charge an initial planning fee, if they charge a percentage for assets under their management and if they make money by selling specific financial products or services. If so, you should follow up by asking how much the service costs. This will give you an idea of how they really make their money and if they have incentive to sell certain products over others. Make sure you understand exactly how you will be charged so there are no surprises down the road if you decide to work with this person.

2. What are the financial services that you and your firm provide? The question within the question here is, "Can you help me achieve my goals?" Some people can only provide you with investment advice, and others are tax consultants. You will likely want to work with someone that provides a complete suite of financial planning services and products that touch on retirement planning, insurance options, legacy and estate structuring, and tax planning. Whatever services they provide, make sure they meet your needs and your anticipated needs.

3. What kinds of clients do you work with the most? A lot of financial professionals work within a niche: retirement planning, risk assessment, life insurance, etc. Finding someone who works with other people that are in the same financial boat as you and who have similar goals can be an important way to make sure they understand your needs. While someone might be a crackerjack annuities cowboy, you might not be interested in that option. Ask follow-up questions that will really help you understand where their expertise lies and whether or not their experience lines up with your needs.

4. How do you approach investing? You may be entirely in the dark about how to approach your investments, or you might have some guiding principles. Either way, ask each candidate what their philosophy is. Some will resonate with you and some won't. A good professional who has a realistic approach to investing won't promise you the moon or tell you that they can make you a lot of money. Professionals who are successful at retirement planning and full service financial management will tell you that they will listen to your goals, risk tolerance and comfort level with different types of investment strategies. Working with someone that you trust is critical, and this question in particular can help you find out who you can and who you can't.

5. How do you remain in contact with your clients? Does your prospective professional hold annual, quarterly or monthly meetings? How often do *you* want to meet with your professional? Some people want to check in once a year, go over everything and make sure their ducks are all in a row. If any changes over the previous year or additions to their legacy planning strategy came up, they'll do it on that date. Other people want a monthly update to be more involved in the decision making process and to understand what's happening with their portfolio. You basically need to determine the right degree of involvement for both you and your financial professional. You'll also want to feel out how your professional communicates. Do you prefer phone calls or face-to-face meetings? Do you want your professional to explain things to you in detail or to summarize for you what decisions they've made? Is the professional willing to give you their direct phone number or their email address? More importantly, do you want that information and do you want to be able to contact them in those ways?

6. Are you my main contact, or do you work with a team? This is another way of finding out how involved with you your professional will be, and how often they will meet with you. It is also a way to discover how the firm they represent operates and manages their clients. Some professionals will answer their own phone, meet with you regularly and have your home phone number on speed dial. Others will meet with you once a year and have a partner or assistant check in with you every quarter to give you an update. Other companies take an entirely team-based approach whereby clients have a main contact but their portfolio is handled by a team of professionals that represent the firm. One way isn't better than another, but one way will be best for you. Find out how the professional you are interviewing operates before entering into an agreement.

7. How do you provide a unique experience for your clients? This is a polite way of asking, "Why should I work with you?" A professional should have a compelling answer to this question that connects with you. Their answer will likely touch on their investment philosophy, their communication style and their expertise. If you hear them describing strengths and philosophies that resonate with you, keep them on your list. Some professionals will tell you that they will make investments with your money that match your values, others will say they will maximize your returns and others will say they will protect your capital while structuring your assets for income. Whatever you're looking for in a professional, you will most likely find it in the answer to this question.

This last question you will want to ask *yourself* after you've met with someone who you are considering hiring:

8. Did they ask questions and show signs that they were interested in working with me? A professional who will structure your assets to reflect your risk tolerance and to position you for a comfortable retirement must be a good listener. You will want to pass by a professional who talks non-stop and tells you what to do without listening to what you want them to do. If you felt they listened well and understood your needs, and seemed interested and experienced in your situation, then they might be right for you.

THE IMPORTANCE OF INDEPENDENCE

Not all firms and financial professionals are created equal. The information in this book has systematically shown that leveraging investments for income and accumulation in today's market requires new ideas and modern planning. In short, you need innovative ideas to come up with the creative solutions that will provide you with the retirement that you want. Innovation thrives on independence. No matter how good a financial professional is, the firm that they represent needs to operate on principles that make sense in today's economy. **Remember, advice about money has been around forever. Good advice, however, changes with the times.**

Timing the market, relying on the sale of stocks for income and banking on high treasury and bond returns are not strategies. They aren't even realistic ways to make money or to generate income. Working with an independent professional can help you break free from the old ways of thinking and position you to create a realistic retirement plan.

Working with an independent professional who relies on fee-based income tied to the success of their performance will also give you greater peace of mind. When you do well, they do well, and that's the way it should be. Your independent financial professional will make sure that:

- Your assets are organized and structured to reflect your risk tolerance.
- Your assets will be available to you when you need them and in the way that you need them.
- You will have a lifetime income that will support your lifestyle through your retirement.
- You are handling your taxes as efficiently as possible.
- Your legacy is in order.
- You have both Need Now and Need Later Money managed in your best interest.
- Your Red Money is turned into Managed Money, and is managed in your best interest.

» Remember Mike and Karen from Chapter 1? Even though they knew they had Social Security benefits coming, they placed some money in savings and each had a pension or a

401(k). **Before they met with a financial professional, they had no idea what their retirement would look like.** *After they met with an independent advisor, they knew exactly what types of assets they had, how much they were worth, how much risk they were exposed to and how they were going to be distributed. They also created an income plan so that they could pay their bills every month the moment they retired, and they maximized their Social Security benefit by targeting the year and month they would get the most lifetime benefits. After their income needs were met, they were able to continue accumulating wealth by investing their extra assets to serve them in the future and contribute to their legacy. Their professional also helped them make decisions that impacted their taxes, protecting the value of their assets and allowing them to keep more of their money.*

This isn't a fairy tale scenario. This is an example of how much you stand to gain by meeting with a financial professional who can help you create a planful approach to your retirement. The concept of Know So and Hope So didn't just apply to their money, it also applied to Mike and Karen. They **hoped** *that they would have enough for retirement and that they had worked hard enough and saved enough to maintain their lifestyle. Working with a financial professional allowed them to* **know** *that their income needs were secured and structured to provide them with income for the rest of their lives and with some money to spare.*

Now, ask yourself: Is your retirement built on hopes and dreams, or a solid, predictable plan?

IT'S WORTH IT!

Finding, interviewing and selecting a financial professional can seem like a daunting task. And honestly, it will take a good amount of work to narrow the field and find the one you want. In the end, it is worth the blood, sweat and tears. Your retirement, lifestyle, assets and legacy is on the line. The choices you make today will have lasting impacts on your life and the life of your loved ones. Working with someone you trust and know you can rely on to make decisions that will benefit you is invaluable. The work it takes to find them is something you will never regret.

CHAPTER 14 CALL TO ACTION //

- Look for a financial professional who puts your needs first. Your goals, objectives, risk tolerance and timeline worries should be the focus of the meeting before they try to offer you any products. A plan is only good if it is a good fit for you and your family.
- Find a professional you can trust by asking family and friends for referrals.
- Make sure to do your due diligence and check out the references of anyone who is recommended to you. Look for resources online such as the Financial Planning Association and the National Association of Personal Financial professionals.
- Interview candidates and make sure you understand how they charge for their services. Look for credentials, licenses and certifications. Ask questions such as: How often do you check in with your clients? May I see a sample of one of your financial plans? And, How do you approach investing? These questions will help ensure that you and your professional are a good fit for each other.
- We hope you enjoyed our book. If you feel we can be of help to you and would like to explore if we can work together, call 1-800-MONEY-SHM (1-800-666-3974) to schedule your interview with us at SHM Financial. We look forward to meeting with you and designing a retirement plan to fit your individual needs.

GLOSSARY[*]

ANNUAL RESET *(ANNUAL RATCHET, CLIQUET)* – Crediting methods measuring index movement over a one year period. Positive interest is calculated and credited at the end of each contract year and cannot be lost if the index subsequently declines. Say that the index increased from 100 to 110 in one year and the indexed annuity had an 80 percent participation rate. The insurance company would take the 10 percent gross index gain for the year (110-100/100), apply the participation rate (10 percent index gain x 80 percent rate) and credit 8 percent interest to the annuity. But, what if in the following year the index declined back to 100? The individual would keep the 8 percent interest earned and simply receive zero interest for the down year. An annual reset structure

---

[*] *"Glossary of Terms." FixedAnnuityFacts.com. NAFA, the National Association for Fixed Annuities, n.d. 12 Nov. 2013*

preserves credited gains and treats negative index periods as years with zero growth.

ANNUITANT – The person, usually the annuity owner, whose life expectancy is used to calculate the income payment amount on the annuity.

ANNUITY – An annuity is a contract issued by an insurance company that often serves as a type of savings plan used by individuals looking for long term growth and protection of assets that will likely be needed within retirement.

AVERAGING – Index values may either be measured from a start point to an end point (point-to-point) or values between the start point and end point may be averaged to determine an ending value. Index values may be averaged over the days, weeks, months or quarters of the period.

BENEFICIARY – A beneficiary is the person designated to receive payments due upon the death of the annuity owner or the annuitant themselves.

BONUS RATE – A bonus rate is the "extra" or "additional" interest paid during the first year (the initial guarantee period), typically used as an added incentive to get consumers to select their annuity policy over another.

CALL OPTION *(ALSO SEE PUT OPTION)* – Gives the holder the right to buy an underlying security or index at a specified price on or before a given date.

CAP – The maximum interest rate that will be credited to the annuity for the year or period. The cap usually refers to the maximum interest credited after applying the participation rate or yield spread. If the index methodology showed a 20 percent increase, the participation rate was 60 percent and the maximum interest cap was 10 percent, the contract would credit 10 percent interest. A few annuities use a maximum gain cap instead of a maximum interest cap with the participation rate or yield spread applied to the lesser of the gain or the cap. If the index methodology showed a 20 percent increase, the participation rate was 60 percent and the maximum gain cap was 10 percent, the contract would credit 6 percent interest.

COMPOUND INTEREST – Interest is earned on both the original principal and on previously earned interest. It is more favorable than simple interest. Suppose that your original principal was $1 and your interest rate was 10 percent for five years. With simple interest, your value is ($1 + $0.10 interest each year) = $1.50. With compound interest, your value is ($1 x 1.10 x 1.10 x 1.10 x 1.10 x 1.10) = $1.61. The advantage of compound interest over simple interest becomes greater as each subsequent period passes.

CREDITING METHOD *(ALSO SEE <u>METHODOLOGY</u>)* – The formula(s) used to determine the excess interest that is credited above the minimum interest guarantee.

DEATH BENEFITS – The payment the annuity owner's estate or beneficiaries will receive if he or she dies before the annuity matures. On most annuities, this is equal to the current account value. Some annuities offer an enhanced value at death via an optional rider that has a monthly or annual fee associated with it.

EXCESS INTEREST – Interest credited to the annuity contract above the minimum guaranteed interest rate. In an indexed annuity the excess interest is determined by applying a stated crediting method to a specific index or indices.

FIXED ANNUITY – A contract issued by an insurance company guaranteeing a minimum interest rate with the crediting of excess interest determined by the performance of the insurer's general account. Index annuities are fixed annuities.

FIXED DEFERRED ANNUITY – With fixed annuities, an insurance company offers a guaranteed interest rate plus safety of your principal and earnings ((subject to the claims-paying ability of the insurance company). Your interest rate will be reset periodically, based on economic and other factors, but is guaranteed to never fall below a certain rate.

FREE WITHDRAWALS – Withdrawals that are free of surrender charges.

INDEX – The underlying external benchmark upon which the crediting of excess interest is based, also a measure of the prices of a group of securities.

IRA *(INDIVIDUAL RETIREMENT ACCOUNT)* – An IRA is a tax-advantaged personal savings plan that lets an individual set aside money for retirement. All or part of the participant's contributions may be tax deductible, depending on the type of IRA chosen and the participant's personal financial circumstances. Distributions from many employer-sponsored retirement plans may be eligible to be rolled into an IRA to continue tax-deferred growth until the funds are needed. An annuity can be used as an IRA; that is, IRA funds can be used to purchase an annuity.

IRA ROLLOVER – IRA rollover is the phrase used when an individual who has a balance in an employer-sponsored retirement plan transfers that balance into an IRA. Such an exchange, when properly handled, is a tax-advantaged transaction.

LIQUIDITY – The ease with which an asset is convertible to cash. An asset with high liquidity provides flexibility, in that the owner can easily convert it to cash at any time, but it also tends to decrease profitability.

MARKET RISK – The risk of the market value of an asset fluctuating up or down over time. In a fixed or fixed indexed annuity, the original principal and credited interest are not subject to market risk. Even if the index declines, the annuity owner would receive no less than their original principal back if they decided to cash in the policy at the end of the surrender period. Unlike a security, indexed annuities guarantee the original premium and the premium is backed by, and is as safe as, the insurance company that issued it (subject to the claims-paying ability of the insurance company).

METHODOLOGY *(ALSO SEE CREDITING METHOD)* – The way that interest crediting is calculated. On fixed indexed annuities, there are a variety of different methods used to determine how index movement becomes interest credited.

MINIMUM GUARANTEED RETURN *(MINIMUM INTEREST RATE)* – Fixed indexed annuities typically provide a minimum guaranteed return over the life of the contract. At the time that the owner chooses to terminate the contract, the cash surrender value is compared to a second value calculated using the minimum guaranteed return and the higher of the two values is paid to the annuity owner.

OPTION – A contract which conveys to its holder the right, but not the obligation, to buy or sell something at a specified price on or before a given date. After this given date the option ceases to exist. Insurers typically buy options to provide for the excess interest potential. Options may be American style whereby they may be exercised at any time prior to the given date, or they may have to be exercised only during a specified window. Options that may only be exercised during a specified period are European-style options.

OPTION RISK – Most insurers create the potential for excess interest in an indexed annuity by buying options. Say that you could buy a share of stock for $50. If you bought the stock and it rose to $60 you could sell it and net a $10 profit. But, if the stock price fell to $40 you'd have a $10 loss. Instead of buying the actual stock, we could buy an option that gave us the right to buy the stock for $50 at any time over the next year. The cost of the option is $2. If the stock price rose to $60 we would exercise our option, buy the stock at $50 and make $10 (less the $2 cost of the option). If the price of the stock fell to $40, $30 or $10, we wouldn't use the option and it would expire. The loss is limited to $2 – the cost of the option.

PARTICIPATION RATE – The percentage of positive index movement credited to the annuity. If the index methodology determined that the index increased 10 percent and the indexed annuity participated in 60 percent of the increase, it would be said that the contract has a 60 percent participation rate. Participation rates may also be expressed as asset fees or yield spreads.

POINT-TO-POINT – A crediting method measuring index movement from an absolute initial point to the absolute end point for a period. An index had a period starting value of 100 and a period ending value of 120. A point-to-point method would record a positive index movement of 20 [120-100] or a 20 percent positive movement [(120-100)/100]. Point-to-point usually refers to annual periods; however the phrase is also used instead of term end point to refer to multiple year periods.

PREMIUM BONUS – A premium bonus is additional money that is credited to the accumulation account of an annuity policy under certain conditions.

PUT OPTION *(ALSO SEE CALL OPTION)* – Gives the holder the right to sell an underlying security or index at a specified price on or before a given date.

QUALIFIED ANNUITIES *(QUALIFIED MONEY)* – Qualified annuities are annuities purchased for funding an IRA, 403(b) tax-deferred annuity or other type of retirement arrangements. An IRA or qualified retirement plan provides the tax deferral. An annuity contract should be used to fund an IRA or qualified retirement plan to benefit from an annuity's features other than tax deferral, including the safety features, lifetime income payout option and death benefit protection.

REQUIRED MINIMUM DISTRIBUTION *(RMD)* – The amount of money that Traditional, SEP and SIMPLE IRA owners and qualified plan participants must begin distributing from their retirement accounts by April 1 following the year they reach age 70.5. RMD amounts must then be distributed each subsequent year.

RETURN FLOOR – Another way of saying minimum guaranteed return.

ROTH IRA – Like other IRA accounts, the Roth IRA is simply a holding account that manages your stocks, bonds, annuities, mutual funds and CD's. However, future withdrawals (including earnings and interest) are typically tax-advantaged once the account has been open for five years and the account holder is age 59.5.

RULE OF 72 – Tells you approximately how many years it takes a sum to double at a given rate. It's handy to be able to figure out, without using a calculator, that when you're earning a 6 percent return, for example, by dividing 6 percent into 72, you'll find that it takes 12 years for money to double. Conversely, if you know it took a sum twelve years to double you could divide 12 into 72 to determine the annual return (6 percent).

SIMPLE INTEREST *(ALSO SEE COMPOUND INTEREST)* – Interest is only earned on the principal balance.

SPLIT ANNUITY – A split annuity is the term given to an effective strategy that utilizes two or more different annuity products – one designed to generate monthly income and the other to restore the original starting principal over a set period of time.

STANDARD & POOR'S 500 *(S&P 500)* – The most widely used external index by fixed indexed annuities. Its objective is to be a benchmark to measure and report overall U.S. stock market performance. It includes a representative sample of 500 common stocks from companies trading on the New York Stock Exchange, American Stock Exchange, and NASDAQ National Market System. The index represents the price or market value of the underlying stocks and does not include the value of reinvested dividends of the underlying stocks.

STOCK MARKET INDEX – A report created from a type of statistical measurement that shows up or down changes in a specific financial market, usually expressed as points and as a percentage, in a number of related markets, or in an economy as a whole (i.e. S&P 500 or New York Stock Exchange).

SURRENDER CHARGE – A charge imposed for withdrawing funds or terminating an annuity contract prematurely. There is no industry standard for surrender charges, that is, each annuity product has its own unique surrender charge schedule. The charge is usually expressed as a percentage of the amount withdrawn prematurely from the contract. The percentage tends to decline over time, ultimately becoming zero.

TRADITIONAL IRA – See <u>IRA (Individual Retirement Account)</u>

TERM END POINT – Crediting methods measuring index movements over a greater timeframe than a year or two. The opposite of an annual reset method. Also referred to as a term point-to-point method. Say that the index value was at 100 on the first day of the period. If the calculated index value was at 150 at the end of the period the positive index movement would be 50 percent (150-100/100). The company would credit a percentage of this movement as excess interest. Index movement is calculated and interest credited at the end of the term and interim movements during the period are ignored.

TERM HIGH POINT *(HIGH WATER MARK)* – A type of term end point structure that uses the highest anniversary index level as the end point. Say that the index value was at 100 on the first day of the period, reached a value of 160 at the end of a contract year during the period, and ended the period at 150. A term high point method would use the 160 value – the highest contract anniversary point reached during the period, as the end point and the gross index gain would be 60 percent (160-100/100). The company would then apply a participation rate to the gain.

TERM YIELD SPREAD – A type of term end point structure which calculates the total index gain for a period, computes the annual compound rate of return deducts a yield spread from the annual rate of return and then recalculates the total index gain for the period based on the net annual rate. Say that an index increased from 100 to 200 by the end of a nine year period. This is the equivalent of an 8 percent compound annual interest rate. If the annuity had a 2 percent term yield spread this would be deducted from the annual interest rate (8 percent-2 percent) and the net rate would be credited to the contract (6 percent) for each of the nine years. Total index gain may also be computed by using the highest anniversary index level as the end point.

VARIABLE ANNUITY – A contract issued by an insurance company offering separate accounts invested in a wide variety of stocks and/or bonds. The investment risk is borne by the annuity owner. Variable annuities are considered securities and require appropriate securities registration.

1035 EXCHANGE – The 1035 exchange refers to the section of tax code that allows annuity owners the flexibility to exchange one annuity for another without incurring any immediate tax liabilities. This action is most often utilized when an annuity holder decides they want to upgrade an annuity to a more favorable one, but they do not want to activate unnecessary tax liabilities that would typically be encountered when surrendering an existing annuity contract.

401(K) ROLLOVER – See <u>IRA Rollover</u>

Made in the USA
Middletown, DE
02 April 2015